EDIBLE GARDENING

for

CALIFORNIA

Vegetables, Herbs, Fruits & Seeds

Jennifer Beaver and Alison Beck

LONE PINE

Lone Pine Publishing International

The Distributor: Lone Pine Publishing
1808 B Street, Suite 140
Auburn, WA USA 98001
Website: www.lonepinepublishing.com

Publisher's Cataloging-In-Publication Data
(Prepared by The Donohue Group, Inc.)

Beaver, Jennifer
    Edible gardening for California / Jennifer Beaver and Alison Beck.

    p. : ill., maps ; cm.

    Includes index.
    ISBN: 978-976-650-049-8

1. Gardening--California 2. Plants, Edible--California. 3. Plant selection--California. I.
Beck, Alison, 1971- II. Title.

SB450.97 .B42 2010
635/.09794

All photos are by Laura Peters and Nanette Samol, except: AAS 163b; Joan de Grey 203b;
Franky de Meyer 35a, 89a; Tamara Eder, 29c, 30, 33bc, 34a, 37a, 40ab, 41, 45b, 80, 93, 155b,
185ab, 191ab, 211a; Elliot Engley 11, 24abc, 25ab; Jennifer Fafard 96, 121a, 229a; Derek Fell
36ab, 53, 54, 55, 57a, 58a, 59ab, 64, 103b, 104, 105, 109a, 115, 127ab, 137a, 139, 141, 163a, 165a,
171a, 183a, 209, 215; Geoffrey Franklyn 63; Saxon Holt, 52, 69, 114, 133, 138, 140, 176, 178,
186, 187ab, 189, 237b; Liz Klose 38, 58b, 73, 83, 88, 117, 223a; Trina Koscielnuk 108; Liza Lau-
zuma 201a; Janet Laughrey 204b; Scott Leigh 101; Heather Markham 45c; Tim Matheson 10,
15, 17, 18b, 19abcd, 20ab, 22bc, 27c, 34b, 39ab, 42b, 43, 44, 45a, 46, 92, 107b, 227ab, 228,
229b; Marilynn McAra 165b; Kim Patrick O'Leary 158, Photos.com 3, 26b, 33a, 57b, 76,
77ab, 78, 85a, 99ab, 241; Robert Ritchie, 37b, 159b; Robert Sproule, 65; Sandy Weatherall
89b, 148; Gary Whyte 62.

Contents

Introduction

Though edible gardens have been part of human culture for thousands of years, there has never been a better time to grow your own food. Gardening interest and information is at an all-time high. As a result, new edible varieties and techniques for home gardens crop up all the time. Our choices are hardier, faster and better-tasting than ever, and plant specialists continue to offer new, compact varieties to meet our need for small-space gardening.

With its abundant sunshine and temperate climate, California is a gardener's paradise. Our problem is not what to grow, but what to choose. California does not offer one-size-fits-all gardening. Larger than many countries and with a wide range of temperatures and climate conditions, California is a checkerboard of microclimates. When you're pulling

up the last of your tomatoes in the north, your cousin in San Diego is just putting in his fall garden. Coastal dwellers may wrestle with grapefruit; over in Palm Springs, grapefruit literally drops from trees.

And that's why you need a guide like this one. Portable, packed with specific information, this book can be as valuable as your favorite hoe or cultivator. It's a garden tool you'll use again and again.

Edibles in the Garden

Why grow edibles? The short answer is, of course, because we want to eat them. But that's only part of it.

There are many reasons to grow edible plants. You'll save money on your grocery bill. You'll save the environment by consuming fewer resources to get food to your table. You'll help wildlife by

Rhubarb and hops grace a sunny corner.

tomatoes. Your beautiful landscape, full of unique and attractive edibles, will be the envy of the neighborhood.

An edible garden includes much more than just vegetables. A multitude of edible fruits, seeds, flowers, trees and herbs will thrive in our gardens. Start by adding a few favorites to patio containers and borders, or design an entire landscape with edibles—the possibilities are endless.

Edible gardening can be extremely satisfying. Pluck a perfect, crunchy sugar snap pea and eat it raw in your own backyard—no trip to the grocery store required. Or watch your child devour a juicy apple from your own tree, knowing exactly where it came from and how it was grown. Every day is a new experience.

It's Easier Than You Think

Many would-be gardeners get discouraged before they begin. They envision the hard, sweaty labor involved in digging large, neat squares and rectangles; removing heavy rocks from the soil; and painstakingly laying out row after row of tiny seeds.

Fast forward to the home garden of the 21st century. While you can certainly

reducing the need to expand cultivated land. By taking control of your own little plot of dirt, you'll get the opportunity to seek out interesting varieties and specialty items so you can dazzle your friends with purple broccoli and Russian

Tomatoes (above), parsley and nasturtiums in a container with annuals (below)

do it the backbreaking traditional way, your friends are using no-dig raised beds and containers. They're putting edibles in back yards, front yards, side yards and balconies, on roofs and driveways and in hanging planters. You can add plenty of edible plants to the landscape you already have. Edibles are everywhere.

How much is enough? That's an individual choice, but it's easy to supplement what you buy by growing a few of your favorites. Two broccoli lovers, for example, will need only three to six plants. Love zucchini? Four zucchini plants—in shapes from round to long and cylindrical—will give you plenty to share with the neighbors.

California Gardening

With more than 160,000 square miles, 58 counties, numerous mountains, deserts, valleys, lakes and coastlines, California has it all. California is an ideal place to grow a huge variety of edible plants. Some plants grow equally well in all parts of the state, and each region favors a select few.

California offers a diverse collection of growing conditions. Gardeners experience almost every imaginable situation somewhere in the state. Recorded temperatures range from -45° to 134° F. One region receives 161" of rain; another gets virtually none. Welcome to California!

Understanding your local geographical region will help you determine what to plant, and when. Keep in mind, however, that conditions can deviate greatly within a region and from garden to garden. Broad factors include climate, season length and day length. Yet individual conditions such as soil type, microclimates, light and heat vary not only from

Peppers (above), beets (below)

Hardiness Zones

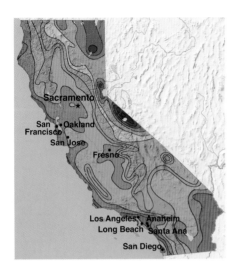

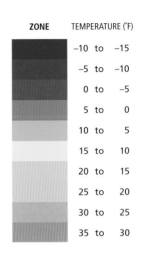

ZONE	TEMPERATURE (°F)
	−10 to −15
	−5 to −10
	0 to −5
	5 to 0
	10 to 5
	15 to 10
	20 to 15
	25 to 20
	30 to 25
	35 to 30

garden to garden but within a single garden. Supplement these general guidelines with local knowledge. Talk to your neighbors and walk around the block. Visit the local garden center and ask lots of questions. Call your local county extension office. Join a local garden club.

Northern California has several distinct geographic areas—coastal, inland valleys, mountains and desert. The northern California coast is the wettest area of the state, with cool days and nights and moderate, even temperatures. Frost is infrequent. Fog influences temperatures and growing conditions during the mostly dry summers from March to November.

Moving inland toward the valley, the fog lifts and temperature becomes more variable. Summers are hotter; winters are colder. The Sierra Nevada mountains block the heavy rains. Across the north, temperatures vary amazingly within a few miles. On a July day in

coastal Half Moon Bay, the temperature could be a pleasant high of 64° F; travel 25 miles inland to Walnut Creek, and the temperature rises 20° F; by the time you go another 25 miles east and stop at Tracy, the temperature is up to 95° F. Know your local weather.

The short, cool summers in parts of northern California present a few challenges. Many "summer" crops (tomatoes, peppers, melons, eggplants) need a long period of warm weather to thrive. By researching short-season varieties, making use of season extenders such as cold frames and cloches, and knowing the microclimates that exist in their own gardens, many gardeners in the northern region succeed with the most finicky warm-season crops.

Some of this region is prime gardening real estate. Between the Sierra Nevada and the coastal mountain ranges lies the 450-mile-long Central Valley, an incredibly fertile area that

Spring and Fall Frost Dates

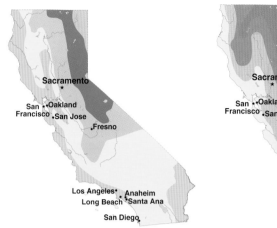

Last Spring Frost Dates

June 1 – June 30

May 1 – May 31

April 1 – April 30

March 1 – March 31

February 1 – February 28

Last Fall Frost Dates

August 1 – August 31

September 1 – September 30

October 1 – October 31

November 1 – November 30

December 1 – December 31

produces more than 350 different crops consumed by the entire country. Home gardeners here enjoy a nine-month growing period ideal for long-season crops.

Southern California also has coastal, mountain, valley and desert conditions. The area is famous worldwide for its ideal climate, and gardeners here plant and harvest nearly year-round, often taking advantage of a second growing season in fall. In many areas, there is no frost from November to January. While northern California sometimes gets too much rain, southern California suffers from too little.

Along the coast, temperatures remain moderate with little fluctuation. Coastal fog keeps things cool but makes it difficult

Marigolds

Raised garden and mulch

to grow sun-lovers like tomatoes and eggplant. Slightly inland, gardeners have a harmonious climate with long, relatively cool, sunny days.

Farther inland, parts of the inland valley stay clear and hot without the marine influence. Temperatures can easily reach 100° F. High heat makes it difficult to grow cool-season crops such as spinach and lettuce. Again, the intrepid local gardeners work with the climate by making smart choices for their individual plots of ground.

To the east lies the desert, a land of limited rainfall and extreme temperatures. Though known for its heat, the desert also gets periods of cold and occasional winter storms.

So how can you make sense of all this for your garden? Get to know these three pieces of climate information: hardiness zone, the last frost date of spring and the first frost date of fall. The hardiness zone is actually a temperature range: plants are rated based on the last zone that offers a decent chance of survival. If you picked up a plant labeled "hardy to

zone 9," for example, you would know that it would do fine in temperatures no lower than 20–30° F, the coldest rating for that zone. If you want to plant it in the colder zone 8, with its lower 10–20° F rating, you would be taking a risk and might need to give the plant some extra care by placing it near a sunny wall or otherwise sheltering it from cold.

Frost dates provide a good estimate of season length (see Spring and Fall Frost Dates map, p. 9). If you can depend on only a few frost-free months, choose plants that will survive a light frost or that will mature during your anticipated growing season. Such plants might be labeled "short season" or "early"; those that require a longer growing season are "long season" or "late." In California, the growing season ranges from a very short 50 days high in the Sierras to a whopping 365 days in parts of southern California. Temperate areas in the Central Valley and along the coast may enjoy from 225 to as many as 300 days before frost effectively ends the growing season.

Cabbages

This information provides a good starting point but should not completely rule your planting decisions. Be flexible. An early, warm spring offers an excellent opportunity to set out a few plants. If spring is cold and wet, however, wait a week or two later than usual.

As with any gardening, growing edible plants should be fun. They add unique colors and textures to your garden and your dinner plate. Experiment with a few each year, and you may find yourself looking for space to add even more.

Special Considerations for California Gardeners

Throughout much of California, fall is wonderful time to plant edibles. The air and earth are still warm, and winter rains provide the only natural irrigation some areas receive all year. While long-season heat lovers such as tomatoes and eggplant might wait till spring, cool-season vegetables such as broccoli, spinach and lettuce are ready to go. Keep this in mind when consulting non-California gardening sources. Many are geared for traditional

spring planting and may not mention our wonderful fall planting season.

Another climate-related issue is the chill factor. Many fruit trees and bushes need a certain number of "chill" hours to produce fruit. A chill hour is defined as 45° F or below. You'll find fruit trees and blueberry bushes ranked high or low chill depending on the number of hours they require. Chill requirements can vary greatly within a small geographic area; check with a nursery specialist to find fruit trees and bushes that will do well in your garden.

Shaping Your Garden

Back when we grew all our own food, farm gardens made sense. The long, neat rows of carefully tended land-consuming crops were necessary to keep families fed.

Today we garden on smaller lots and often need to wedge a tomato or parsley plant into what we already have. Fortunately, it's not difficult. There are an unlimited number of ways to integrate edibles into existing ground-level beds. Create a cottage-style garden, with vegetables planted in groups and drifts. Tuck

Lettuce (above), red cabbage (below)

in groups of vegetables to make a formal or informal pattern, depending on the look you desire. In short, treat your edibles like ornamentals.

Or consider raised beds, an alternative no-dig solution to creating more gardening space. Beautiful and functional, the French potager, or kitchen garden, consists of a symmetrical arrangement of raised beds. Rather than confining one plant to one bed, vegetables, herbs and fruits and flowers mix it up in a harmonious and lovely blend.

Co-mingling plants is not only beautiful, but healthy. Variety reduces pests and

diseases because it limits the number of susceptible plants in close proximity.

Another option for raised beds is square-foot gardening. Dividing an area into square-foot increments provides a higher yield and neater garden. A 4 x 4' raised bed, for example, creates 16 smaller planting squares. In each square, plant as much of a single crop as the space will allow. Space-hogs like tomato and zucchini will each fill a whole square. Smaller plants like radishes flourish 16 to a square. After harvesting, plant something new. Experiment by plotting it out on a sheet of graph paper.

Gardeners have embraced container gardening because of its ease and versatility. Many fruits, vegetables and herbs grow successfully in containers on a balcony, porch, patio or deck. If you don't have room for trailing vines to spread, consider a trellis or obelisk and grow vines up instead of out. Many of the same vine-forming plants that grow up trellises will also trail nicely over the edge of a hanging basket. Even if you have abundant space, containers offer

Scarlet runner beans make lovely climbing plants.

convenience and make wonderful accents sprinkled among the more permanent plantings.

Both raised beds and containers have the added advantage of fresh dirt and no digging. They remove barriers to edible gardening.

As your garden grows and develops and you need to add new plants, think about adding edibles. Need a new shrub? Consider a raspberry or blueberry bush. Train peas and nasturtiums up an obelisk. Grow grapes across your pergola. Espalier an apple tree across a sunny side wall. The possibilities are only limited by your imagination.

Edible plants have tremendous ornamental value. Once relegated to different sections of the yard, edibles and ornamentals happily share space, and our gardens are the better for it. Edible plants vary in size, color and texture and often have wonderful flowers, stunning foliage or decorative fruit in colors

and shapes not often replicated in our ornamental plants. When you look at an edible plant, don't just think about the end result; think about the appearance of the plant and what it can add to your ornamental garden.

Take advantage of stunning foliage. Colors range from gray-green and greens so dark they're almost black to shades of red, purple, yellow, blue and bronze. Richly patterned and veined foliage sometimes contrasts with the leaf color. Foliage can be immense or delicate and feathery.

Edibles with Interesting Foliage
Amaranth
Artichokes
Asparagus
Cabbage
Carrots
Chard
Cilantro
Fennel
Fiddlehead Ferns
Kale
Leeks
Lettuce

Mustard
Rhubarb
Squash

Getting Started

Finding the right mix of edibles for your garden requires experimentation and creativity. Before you start planting, consider the growing conditions such as light, soil, exposure and frost tolerance in your garden. Plants will be healthier and have fewer problems if grown in optimum conditions.

Make a sketch to help you visualize how various conditions can affect your planting decisions. Note shaded areas, low-lying or wet areas, exposed or windy sections, etc. Understanding your garden's growing conditions will help you learn where plants perform best and prevent costly and frustrating planning mistakes.

Light

There are four basic levels of light in a garden: full sun, partial shade (partial sun), light shade and full shade. Buildings, trees, fences and the position of the

Raised bed in full sun

sun at different times of the day and year affect available light. Knowing what light is available in your garden will help you determine where to place each plant.

Plants in full sun locations, such as along south-facing walls, receive more than six hours of direct sunlight in a single day. Locations classified as partial shade, such as east- or west-facing walls, receive direct sunlight for part of the day (four to six hours) and shade for the rest. Light shade locations receive shade for most or all of the day, though some sunlight does filter through to ground level. An example of a light shade location might be the ground under a small-leaved tree such as a birch. Full shade locations, which can include the north side of a house, receive no direct sunlight.

Plant your edibles where they will grow best. If your garden has hot, dry areas or low-lying damp places, select plants that prefer those conditions. Experimenting will help you learn about the conditions of your garden.

Sunflowers tolerate a range of soil conditions.

Soil

Soil quality is an extremely important element of a healthy garden. Roots rely on the air, water and nutrients held within the soil. Of course, plants also depend on soil to hold them upright. Plants benefit soil as well by breaking down large clumps, binding small particles to prevent erosion and reducing the amount of exposed surface. When plants die and break down, they add organic nutrients to soil and feed beneficial microorganisms.

Soil is made up of different-sized particles. Sand is the largest; water drains quickly from sandy soil, and nutrients tend to get washed away. Sandy soil does not compact easily because the large particles leave air pockets between them.

Clay particles, the smallest, can be seen only through a microscope. Clay holds the most nutrients, but it also compacts easily and has little air space. Clay is slow to absorb water and equally slow to let it drain. Silt is midway between sand and clay in particle size. Most soils are a combination of sand, clay and silt and are called loams.

When planting intensively, keep plants fairly close together but leave enough room for each to grow. Many edibles go from small seedlings to large mature plants very quickly. Give them some room to spread and increase your yield.

Soil's pH level (the scale on which acidity or alkalinity is measured) also influences the availability of nutrients. Most plants thrive in soil with a pH between 5.5 and 7.5. Reduce soil acidity by adding horticultural lime or wood ashes; increase it with sulfur, peat moss or pine needles. For plants that prefer a pH that varies greatly from that of your garden soil, use planters or create raised beds where it is easier to control and alter the pH level of soil.

Consider buying testing kits from a garden center or sending a soil sample to a soil-testing lab. In addition to analyzing the pH and nutrients, some soil tests will also reveal the presence of industrial or chemical pollutants. These are of particular concern when growing edibles because the plants may absorb them and we eat them. If your garden soil is too toxic for edibles, grow them in raised beds or containers.

Soil type and terrain also affect drainage. Plants that prefer well-drained soil and do not require a large amount of moisture grow well on a hillside garden with rocky soil. Improve water retention in these areas by adding organic matter.

Water-loving plants are ideal for low-lying areas that retain water for longer periods. Improve drainage by adding gravel, creating raised beds or using French drains or drainage tile.

Exposure

Your garden is exposed to wind, heat, cold and rain. Some plants are better adapted than others to withstand the potential damage of these forces. Buildings, walls, fences, hills, hedges, trees and even tall perennials influence and often reduce exposure.

Wind and heat are the elements most likely to cause damage. Both can rob plants of much-needed moisture. In areas of low rainfall, it's particularly important to monitor their effect. The sun can be very intense, and heat rises quickly on a sunny afternoon. Choose edibles that tolerate or even thrive in hot weather for your garden's hot spots.

Too much rain can damage plants, as can over-watering. Mulch early in the season, to help prevent seeds or seedlings from being washed away in heavy rain. Most established plants beaten down by heavy rain will recover, but some are

Open spaces expose plants to stronger wind.

slower to do so. Waterlogged soil encourages root rot. Most edible plants prefer well-drained soil.

Hanging baskets are particularly susceptible to wind and heat exposure, losing water from the soil surface and the leaves. Hanging baskets look wonderful, but watch for wilting, and water the baskets regularly to keep them looking great. New water-holding polymers that hold water and release it as the soil dries have been developed for use in soil mixes.

Frost Tolerance

When planting edibles, consider their ability to tolerate an unexpected frost. Most gardeners here can expect a chance of frost until mid- to late May, though warmer areas may have a last frost date in April and colder areas in June. The map on p. 9 gives a general idea of when you can expect your last frost date. Your local garden center should be able to provide more precise information. While frost is an infrequent issue in the south, it can devastate tropicals and other frost-tender plants.

Edible plants are grouped into three categories based on how tolerant they are of cold weather: hardy, half-hardy or tender.

Hardy plants can tolerate low temperatures and even frost. They can be planted in the garden early and may survive long into fall or even winter. They often fade in summer heat after producing an early crop. Many hardy edibles are sown directly in the garden in the weeks before the last frost date and can be sown again in summer for a second crop in fall.

Half-hardy plants tolerate a light frost but will be killed by a heavy one. These edibles can be planted out around the

Mulched garden

last frost date and will generally benefit from being started indoors from seed if they are slow to mature.

Tender plants have no frost tolerance and might suffer if the temperature drops to even a few degrees above freezing. They are often started early indoors and are not planted in the garden until the last frost date has passed and the ground has had a chance to warm up. These edibles often tolerate hot summer temperatures.

Protecting plants from frost is relatively simple. Cover plants overnight with sheets, towels, burlap or even cardboard boxes—don't use plastic because it doesn't provide any insulation.

Peas prefer cold weather and will tolerate spring frosts.

Choosing what to grow provides year-round entertainment. Plan now for next year; seek out unusual varieties of some of your favorites. Select plants and cultivars suitable for your climate and conditions. For example, avoid pumpkin, which needs four or five months to mature, if you have a short growing season.

Tuck nasturtiums among the lettuce.

Preparing the Garden

Take time to properly prepare your growing area. You'll save time, reduce effort and get better food. Get edibles off to a good start by minimizing weeds and adding organic material.

Tackle a garden bed by loosening soil with a large garden fork and removing weeds. Avoid working very wet or very dry soil; it breaks down air and water pockets and you will damage the soil, making it less fertile. Add good quality compost and work it in using a spade, fork or rototiller. How much compost will you need? Plan on covering your garden with a 2–4" layer. For container gardens and raised beds, use potting soil. When used in containers, regular garden soil loses its structure and quickly compacts into a solid, poorly draining mass.

Or do it the easy way and create a no-dig lasagna garden. The name has nothing to do with the Italian pasta dish and everything to do with layering. It's fast, organic and easy on the back. First, stake out your garden area. Cover it with cardboard or pads of newspaper to smother the grass. Soak it with water. Next, start your layers: 2–3" of coir or peat moss followed by 2–3" of organic material such as mulch, compost or grass clippings. Repeat until the pile reaches 18–24". Soak your new gardening bed, and top with mulch. You can plant immediately or let it simmer for awhile to decompose.

Organic matter is a small but important component that benefits all soil types. Used with sandy soil, for example, it increases water and nutrient absorptions while binding the large particles. In clay soil, organic matter increases the water-absorbing and draining potential

Compostable materials (above), bin (top right), red wigglers (bottom right)

by opening up spaces between the tiny particles. Common organic additives include grass clippings, shredded leaves, peat moss, chopped straw and well-rotted manure.

Composting

Making your own compost is simple, convenient and uses up a lot of household waste that would eventually wind up in landfill. Start with a purchased or homemade pile or bin. In this controlled environment, organic matter can be fully broken down before being introduced to your garden. Organic material includes such things as leaves, grass, kitchen vegetable scraps and coffee grounds. Good composting methods also reduce the possibility of spreading pests and diseases.

What's so great about compost? The decomposition process results in an all-natural additive chockfull of beneficial nutrients and helpful organisms that will do wonders for your garden. Why

not use fresh material straight from your kitchen or lawnmower bag? The microorganisms that break down fresh organic material use the same nutrients as your plants. Fresh organics essentially cannibalize your gardening efforts. As they break down they rob your plants of vital nutrients, particularly nitrogen. Also, fresh organic matter and garden debris might encourage or introduce pests and diseases to your garden.

Creating compost is easy. You can speed up the process by following a few simple guidelines:
• Put in both dry and fresh materials. Use mostly dry matter such as chopped straw, shredded leaves or sawdust. Fresh green matter, such as vegetable scraps, grass clippings or pulled weeds, breaks down quickly and produces nitrogen, which feeds the decomposer organisms while they break down the tougher dry matter.

• Alternate the green and dry and mix in small amounts of garden soil or finished compost—it will introduce beneficial microorganisms. If the pile seems very dry, sprinkle on some water—the compost should be moist but not soaking wet, like a wrung-out sponge.

• Aerating speeds decomposition, so turn the pile or poke holes in it every week or two. A well-aerated compost pile gener-

ates a lot of heat. Temperatures can reach 160° F or more. Such high temperatures destroy weed seeds and kill many damaging organisms. Most beneficial organisms are not killed until the temperature rises higher than 160° F. Some gardeners monitor the temperature near the middle of the pile with a thermometer attached to a long probe, similar to a large meat thermometer. Turning compost when the temperature reaches 160° F stimulates the heat process, but prevents the temperature from becoming high enough to kill beneficial organisms.

• Don't put diseased or pest-ridden materials into your compost pile. If the damaging organisms are not destroyed, they could spread throughout your garden.

• When you can no longer recognize what you put into the compost bin, and the temperature no longer rises upon turning, your compost is ready to be mixed into your garden beds. Getting to this point can take as little as one month.

Compost can also be purchased from most garden centers.

Selecting Edible Plants

Many gardeners consider the trip to their local garden center an important rite of spring. Big-box retailers and garden centers increasingly stock interesting fruits, vegetables and trees along with old standbys. Others gardeners find it rewarding to start their own plants from seed. They take great delight in hunting down new and heirloom varieties online and swapping seeds with like-minded friends.

Both methods have benefits. Purchased plants provide immediate gratification and the relative assurance of healthy stock. For those without the time, space or inclination to start seeds, it's worth the extra expense to buy a six-pack of eggplant or a gallon tomato. On the other hand, starting from seed offers you a far greater selection of species and varieties. Learn how to do it on p. 23.

When browsing for plants and seeds, you'll find references to the terms hybrid and heirloom. Hybrids are generally newer selections been bred for specific traits such as flavor, size, disease resistance or improved storability. Often developed for market growers and food exporters, hybrids usually have traits that make them suitable for packing and transporting long distances without

Lemon cucumber is a tasty heirloom.

Healthy plants (left), unhealthy plants (above)

Cutting roots before planting

spoiling. Hybrids rarely come true to type from collected seed.

Heirloom refers to plant selections cultivated for generations. Many gardeners like the connection with history, knowing that their grandparents grew the same plant. Some of the most intriguing vegetable selections are heirlooms, and advocates say they are the tastiest and most resistant to pests and diseases. Seeds collected from the plants produce true-to-type offspring.

Purchased plants grow in a variety of containers. Some are sold in individual pots, some in divided cell-packs and others in undivided trays. Each type has advantages and disadvantages.

Plants in individual pots are usually well established and generally have plenty of space for root growth. Most likely seeded in flat trays, then transplanted into individual pots, they are expensive owing to the cost of labor, pots and soil.

Plants grown in cell-packs are often inexpensive and hold several plants, making them easy to transport. Because each cell is quite small, it doesn't take long for a plant to become root-bound.

Plants grown in undivided trays have plenty of room for root growth and can be left in the trays longer than in other types of containers. Their roots tend to tangle, making the plants difficult to separate.

Regardless of the container, check the roots. If they're emerging from the container bottom or are wrapped around the inside of the container in a thick web, they've been in there too

Sunflower seeds (left), nwasturtium seeds (right)

long. Such plants are slow to establish once transplanted.

What should you watch for when shopping? Look for compact plants with good color. Healthy leaves are firm and vibrant; unhealthy leaves may be wilted, chewed or discolored. Tall, leggy plants have usually been deprived of light. Avoid sickly plants. At best, they won't perform as well as the healthy ones. At worst, they may spread pests or diseases.

When you bring plants home, water them if they are dry. Plants in small containers may require water more than once a day. Begin to harden them off so they can be transplanted into the garden as soon as possible. Hardening off is the process that allows your sheltered, greenhouse-grown plants to become accustomed to the outdoors. Place them in a lightly shaded spot each day and bring them in to a sheltered porch, garage or house each night for about a week to acclimatize them to your garden.

Starting Edibles from Seed

Dozens of catalogs offer edible plants to start from seed. Many gardeners spend their chilly winter evenings poring through seed catalogs and planning their spring, summer and fall gardens. Also check out the internet, garden centers and seed exchange groups.

Starting from seed saves money, particularly if you want a lot of plants. The basic equipment is not expensive, and a simple sunny window provides a good launching area. Keep in mind that you may run out of room quickly if you enthusiastically plant more than two trays.

Each plant in this book is accompanied by specific seed-starting information. Here are some general guidelines.

There are several options when selecting seed-starting containers. Cell-packs

in trays with plastic dome covers are very easy. The cell-packs keep roots separated, and the tray and dome keep moisture in.

Other choices include regular ceramic or plastic pots, peat pots or peat pellets. Peat pots and pellets are particularly easy because you stick them in the ground along with your new seedling, without disturbing the roots.

Use a sterilized growing mix (soil mix) intended for seedlings. Made from peat moss, vermiculite and perlite, they have advanced water-holding capabilities that help them stay moist while draining appropriately. Among other advantages, soil mixes prevent damping off, which is caused by soil-borne fungi. The affected seedling looks like it has been pinched at soil level. The pinched area blackens, and the seedling topples over and dies. Using sterile soil mix, keeping soil evenly moist and maintaining good air circulation will prevent plants from damping off.

Fill pots or seed trays with soil mix and firm slightly. Soil too firmly packed will not drain well. Before planting, wet the soil to prevent seeds from getting washed around. Plant large seeds one or two to a cell. Place smaller seeds in a folded piece of paper and sprinkle evenly over the soil. Mix tiny seeds with fine sand and sprinkle on the soil surface. Follow seed packet directions for planting depth.

Additional light keeps plants healthy indoors.

While seeds are germinating, place pots or flats in plastic bags to retain humidity. Many planting trays come with clear plastic covers that keep in moisture. Once seeds have germinated, remove the cover.

Water seeds and small seedlings gently with a fine spray from a hand-held mister—a strong spray can easily wash small seeds away.

Seeds provide all the energy and nutrients that young seedlings require. Small seedlings do not need to be fertilized until they have about four or five true leaves. When the first leaves begin to shrivel, the plant has used up all its seed energy, and you can use a fertilizer diluted to quarter strength.

If seedlings get too big for their containers before you're ready to plant, move them to slightly larger containers to avoid confining the roots. Harden plants off by exposing them to outdoor conditions for longer every day for at least a week before planting them.

Potting up gives seedlings room to grow.

Why start seeds early indoors? It extends the growing season. In some areas, garden-planted seeds won't have a chance to mature before frost hits. Older seedlings, on the other hand, get a head start.

Edibles to Start Indoors

This list is for people with a short growing season; southern California gardeners and others with longer temperature weather can direct sow these plants.

Artichokes
Broccoli and other *Brassica* spp.
Celery
Cucumbers
Eggplant
Leeks
Melons
Okra
Peppers
Squash
Tomatoes
Watermelons

When you plant seeds directly in the garden, the procedure is similar. Begin with a well-prepared, smoothly raked bed. The small furrows left by the rake help hold moisture and prevent seeds from being washed away. Sprinkle the seeds onto the soil and cover them lightly with peat moss or more soil. To ensure even germination, keep the soil moist using a gentle spray. Cover your newly seeded bed with chicken wire, an old sheet or some thorny branches to discourage pets from digging.

Cucumber (top), watermelon (center), broccoli (bottom)

Large seeds are easy to see, sow and plant. Small seeds are a little trickier; because it's harder to determine placement, you may need to thin crops as they emerge. Pull out the weaker plants when groups look crowded. Use the thinnings from lettuce, spinach and others in a salad or stir-fry.

Edibles for Direct Seeding
Amaranth
Beans
Beets
Carrots
Chard
Coriander
Corn
Lettuce
Nasturtiums
Parsley
Peas
Quinoa
Radishes
Sunflowers

Beets

Lettuce

Radishes

Sunflower

Growing Edibles

Once your plants have hardened off, it is time to plant them out. If your beds are already prepared, you are ready to start. The only tool you are likely to need is a trowel. Set aside enough time to complete the job; young plants will dry and die if left out in the sun. Try to choose an overcast day for planting.

Planting

Plants are easier to remove from their containers if the soil is moist. Push on the bottom of the cell to ease them out. If the roots have grown together, free them by gently untangling by hand or immersing them in water and washing away some of the soil. If you must handle the plant, hold it by a leaf to avoid crushing the stems. Remove and discard any damaged leaves or growth.

The root ball should contain a network of white plant roots. If it is densely matted and twisted, break the tangles apart with your thumbs. New root growth will start from the breaks, allowing the plant to spread outward.

Plants started in peat pots and peat pellets can be planted pot and all. When planting peat pots into the garden, remove the top 1½–2½" of the pot. If any of the pot is sticking up out of the soil, it can wick moisture away from your plant.

Insert your trowel into the soil and pull it toward you, creating a wedge. Place your plant into the hole and firm the soil around it with your hands. Water gently but thoroughly. Until it is established, the plant will need regular watering.

Some of the plants in this book are sold in large containers. In a prepared bed, dig a hole that will accommodate the root ball. Fill the hole in gradually, settling the soil with water as you go.

Other plants are sold as bare roots or crowns, or in moistened peat moss, sphagnum moss or sawdust. Shake off any packing material and soak these plants in water for a few hours before planting. Be sure to accommodate the roots; spread them out in a hole big enough to hold them without crowding.

A few plants are sold as bulbs, such as garlic and onion sets. Plant them about three times as deep as the bulb is high.

More detailed planting instructions are given, as needed, in the plant accounts.

Planting Trees

Many California gardeners consider fruit trees an essential part of their edible landscape. Consistently trimmed to a reasonable height that allows easy access to the fruit, they add stature, dimension and deliciousness without overwhelming the available gardening space.

After you've purchased your container-grown or bare-root tree, you'll want to get it into the ground as soon as possible. Start by digging a hole about as deep as the root ball and about three times as wide. If you're working with a bare-root tree, spread the roots out. Before settling your tree in its new home, make sure it's planted at the right height. Look for the root flare, the area where the roots spread out from the tree base. To allow for proper root development, the root flare should be slightly above the soil level.

Once you're happy with the placement, fill in the hole, tapping the dirt down to eliminate air pockets. Mulch, keeping it 2–3" from the tree. Water thoroughly; keep the area moist but not saturated.

Weeding

Controlling weeds keeps the garden healthy and neat. Weeds compete for

Mulch keeps weeds at bay.

light, nutrients and space, and they can also harbor pests and diseases.

Pull weeds by hand or use a hoe to scuff across the surface and uproot or sever weeds. The best time is shortly after it rains, when the soil is soft and damp. Try to pull weeds while they are still small. Once they are large enough to flower, many will quickly set seed; then you will have an entire new generation to worry about.

Mulching

Until recently, no one said much about mulch. Now it's all the rage—we've discovered its ability to keep the soil moist and maintain consistent soil temperatures. In areas that receive heavy wind or rainfall, mulch protects soil and prevents erosion. Put a layer around your plants to reduce weed germination.

Effective in beds, planters and containers, mulches come in many varieties. Organic mulches such as compost, grass clippings or shredded leaves add nutrients as they break down. They improve the quality of the soil and, ultimately, the health of your plants. Avoid colored or large chunks of bark; they decompose slowly, if at all, and may contain chemicals that will not help your soil.

Spread about 2–4" of mulch over the soil after you have finished planting, or spread your mulch first and then make spaces to plant afterward. Don't pile it near plant stems and crowns where it can trap moisture, prevent air circulation and encourage fungal disease. Replenish your mulch as it breaks down.

Watering

Owing to a severe water shortage throughout much of the state, California gardeners are learning to be water smart. That means using efficient tools like drip watering systems and moisture meters. To conserve water and grow healthy plants, water when your plants need it—not when you get around to it. Automated systems have many advantages but they are no substitute for personally checking individual plants on an ongoing basis. Just make it part of your weeding, deadheading and produce-picking routine.

How you water is equally important. Whenever possible, avoid wetting leaves. Wet leaves, fruit and vegetables attract fungal and other diseases. Keep the moisture at the base of the plant. Timing is important, too. Water during the day to give the sun a chance to burn off excess moisture.

All plants have different watering requirements, and those are spelled out in the individual listings. Many appreciate thorough but infrequent irrigation to develop deep roots. In a dry spell, they will seek out water trapped deep in the ground. Those that get a light daily sprinkle develop roots that stay close to the soil surface, making the plants vulnerable to heat and dry spells. Use mulch to prevent water from evaporating out of the soil.

Other plants have roots that naturally stay close to the surface. They will need more frequent water to keep the roots

A soaker hose applies deeply penetrating water with less evaporation and run-off than a sprinkler.

from drying out. For greatest efficiency, plant deep-root and shallow-root plants close together.

Plants in containers, hanging baskets and planters need watering more frequently than in-ground plants—even twice daily during hot, sunny weather. The smaller the container, the more often the plants will need water.

Fertilizing

We demand a lot from our edible plants. Many are annuals, and we expect them to grow and produce a good crop of fruit or vegetables in only one season. They, in return, demand a lot of sun, nutrients and water. Mixing plenty of compost into the soil is a good start, but fertilizing regularly can make a big difference when it comes to harvest your crop.

Whenever possible, use organic fertilizers. They do double duty by feeding your plants and improving your soil. Find them online or at your local garden center. Follow the directions carefully—

Soaker hose arranged on a raised bed.

using too much can kill your plants by burning their roots and may upset the soil's microbial balance, allowing pathogens to move in or dominate.

Fertilizer comes in many forms. Liquids or water-soluble powders are easiest to use when watering. Slow-release pellets or granules are mixed into the garden or potting soil or are sprinkled around the plant.

Decoding Garden Language

Throughout the guide, we've used commonly used garden phrases to describe various situations and conditions. Need some clarification? Here are more in-depth explanations of a few that may seem perplexing:

Drought tolerant once established

Given our water shortage, Californians are always on the hunt for something that tolerates drought. Drought tolerant means that the plant will grow well with little supplemental water. But here's the tricky part: In many areas of California, the only time we get natural water—or rain—is in winter. That means a plant may need to go three seasons without water to be considered truly drought tolerant. Pretty tough. The other consideration is the "until established" part. To be on the safe side, water a "drought-tolerant" plant

regularly the first year as it gets established. After that, determine watering requirements by observing behavior: Is it stressed? Drooping? Dropping leaves? Becoming a bug or disease magnet? All of these may be signs that it needs water.

Soil should be humus rich, moist and well drained

The humus part means that you should work a lot of compost into the soil before planting. In addition to providing nutrients, the compost also helps with watering needs. It holds water so the soil stays moist; and it drains well so your plants don't rot in water-logged soil. Moist but well-drained soil feels like a wrung-out sponge.

In warm-winter regions; in cold-winter regions

As we mentioned earlier, California has an amazing number of climate zones and microclimates. They're difficult to sort out geographically, so we can't say, "North of Santa Barbara, do this," or some other helpful phrase. To get the most out of the plant guide, be aware of your own little corner of the world. In general, warm-winter areas are those with little or light frost that offer many months of steady warm weather. Cold-winter regions have frost and shorter growing seasons.

Organic amendments (left to right): moisture-holding granules, earthworm castings, glacial dust, mycorrhizae, bat guano, compost, bone meal and coir fiber.

Problems and Pests

New annual edible plants are planted each spring, and you may choose to plant different species each year. Changing and adding new varieties makes it difficult for pests and diseases to find their preferred host plants and establish a population. However, because many edibles are closely related, any problems are likely to attack all the plants in the same family. Pests that love your broccoli will also be enamored of your cauliflower, for example.

Beneficial bugs: lacewing (top), ladybug (center), ladybug larvae (below).

For many years, pest control meant spraying or dusting with the goal of eliminating every pest in the landscape. Today's more moderate approach is IPM (Integrated Pest Management or Integrated Plant Management), a sort of live-and-let-live policy. The goal of IPM is to reduce pest problems so only negligible damage is done. Of course, you must determine what degree of damage is acceptable to you. Consider whether a pest's damage is localized or covers the

Borage flowers attract beneficial insects.

entire plant. Will the damage kill the plant or is it affecting only the outward appearance? Are there methods of controlling the pest without chemicals?

A good IPM program includes learning about the conditions your plants need for healthy growth, which pests might affect your plants, where and when to look for those pests and how to control them. Keep records of pest damage because your observations can reveal patterns useful in spotting recurring problems and in planning your maintenance regime.

There are four steps in effective and responsible pest management. Cultural controls are the most important and are the first response when problems arise. Use physical controls next, followed by biological controls. Resort to chemical controls only when the first three possibilities have been exhausted.

Cultural controls are simply the day-to-day techniques you use to care of your garden. Keeping your plants as healthy as possible is the best defense against pests. Growing plants in the conditions they prefer and keeping your

soil healthy by adding plenty of organic matter are just two of the cultural controls you can use to keep pests manageable. Choose disease-resistant varieties to minimize problems. Space plants to provide good air circulation and reduce stress caused by competition for light, nutrients and space. Take plants that are destroyed by the same pests every year out of the landscape. Remove diseased foliage and branches, and burn or take them to a permitted dumpsite. Prevent the spread of disease by keeping gardening tools clean and by tidying up fallen leaves and dead plant matter at the end of every growing season.

Physical controls are generally used to combat insect problems. They include picking them off by hand, using barriers and installing traps that catch or confuse them. Physical control of disease may require removing the infected plant or plant part to keep the problem from spreading.

Biological controls use predators that prey on pests. Animals such as birds, snakes, frogs, spiders, lady beetles and certain bacteria can play an important role in keeping pest populations manageable. Encourage these creatures to take up permanent residence in your garden. A birdbath and birdfeeder allow birds to enjoy your yard and feed on a wide variety of insect pests. Many beneficial insects are probably already living in your landscape, and you can encourage them to stay by planting appropriate food sources. Herbs such as parsley, thyme and oregano attract beneficial insects.

Chemical controls should rarely be necessary, but if you must use them, there are some "organic" options available. Organic and chemical sprays are dangerous, but organics break down

Brussels sprouts (above), kohlrabi (below)

Crop rotation is one of the most effective methods of disease-reducing methods. Don't put the same plant, or even one from the same family, in the same location two years in a row. By changing the crop from year to year, you can prevent problems from setting in annually. Wait two years before planting any member of a family in the same location (the Brassica *family, for example, includes broccoli, Brussels sprouts, cabbage, cauliflower, collards, horseradish, kale, kohlrabi, mustard, oriental cabbage, radish, rutabaga and turnip).*

into harmless compounds. Traditional chemicals linger in the garden and may have long-lasting negative effects. Both organic and traditional chemicals may also kill the beneficial insects you have been trying to attract to your garden. Organic chemicals are available at most garden centers.

Follow the manufacturer's instructions carefully. A large amount of pesticide is no more effective than the recommended amount. Note that if a particular pest is not listed on the package, that product will not control that pest. Proper and early identification of pests is vital to finding a quick solution.

Cultural, physical, biological and chemical controls provide defenses against insects, but diseases can only be controlled culturally. Not surprisingly, healthy plants fight off illness, though some diseases can infect plants regardless of their level of health. Prevention is key. Once a plant has been infected, consider destroying it to prevent the disease from spreading.

Insect damage disfigures asparagus spears (left); healthy spears (right) are more appetizing.

Aphids

Beetles

Alphabetical Guide to Pests and Diseases

Anthracnose

Fungus; yellow or brown spots on leaves; sunken lesions and blisters on stems; can kill plant.

What to do: choose resistant varieties and cultivars; keep soil well drained; thin out stems to improve air circulation; avoid handling wet foliage; remove and destroy infected plant parts; clean up and destroy debris from infected plants at end of growing season.

Aphids

Tiny, pear-shaped, green, black, brown, red or gray insects; can be winged or wingless, e.g., woolly adelgids. Cluster along stems, on buds and on leaves; suck sap from plant; cause distorted or stunted growth; sticky honeydew forms on plant surfaces and encourages sooty mold growth.

What to do: squish small colonies by hand; dislodge with brisk water spray; encourage predatory insects and birds that feed on aphids; spray serious infestations with insecticidal soap or neem oil according to package directions.

Aster Yellows

see Viruses

Bacillus thuringiensis (B.t.)

A biological control that breaks down the gut lining of caterpillars.

Beetles

Many types and sizes; usually rounded in shape with hard, shell-like outer wings covering membranous inner wings. Some are beneficial, e.g., ladybird beetles ("ladybugs"); others, e.g., Japanese beetles, leaf skeletonizers and weevils, eat plants. Larvae: see Borers, Grubs. Leave wide range of chewing damage: make small or large holes in or around margins of leaves; consume entire leaves or areas between leaf veins ("skeletonize"); may also chew holes in flowers. Some bark beetle species carry deadly plant diseases.

Borer damage on squash

What to do: pick beetles off at night and drop them into an old coffee can half filled with soapy water (soap prevents them from floating and climbing out).

Blight

Fungal diseases. Many types; e.g., leaf blight, needle blight, snow blight. Leaves, stems and flowers blacken, rot and die.

What to do: thin stems to improve air circulation; keep mulch away from base of plants; remove debris from garden at end of growing season; remove and destroy infected plant parts.

Borers

Larvae of some moths, wasps and beetles. Worm-like; vary in size and get bigger as they bore through plants; among the most damaging plant pests. Burrow into plant stems, branches, leaves and/or roots; destroy vascular tissue (plant veins and arteries) and structural strength; weaken stems to cause breakage; leaves will wilt; may see tunnels in leaves, stems or roots; rhizomes may be hollowed out entirely or in part.

What to do: may be able to squish borers within leaves; remove and destroy bored parts; may need to dig up and destroy infected roots and rhizomes.

Bugs (True Bugs)

Green, brown, black or brightly colored and patterned, small insects, up to ½" long. Many are beneficial; a few pests, such as lace bugs, pierce plants to suck out sap; toxins may be injected that deform plants; sunken areas remain where pierced; leaves rip as they grow; leaves, buds and new growth may be dwarfed and deformed.

What to do: remove debris and weeds from around plants in fall to destroy over-wintering sites. Spray plants with insecticidal soap or neem oil according to package directions.

Case Bearers
see Caterpillars

Caterpillars

Larvae of butterflies, moths, sawflies; include bagworms, budworms, case

Lygus bug on cosmos flower

bearers, cutworms, leaf rollers, leaf tiers and loopers. Chew foliage and buds; can completely defoliate a plant if infestation is severe.

What to do: removal from plant is best control; use high-pressure water and soap, or pick caterpillars off small plants by hand. Control biologically using the naturally occurring soil bacterium *Bacillus thuringiensis* var. *kurstaki* or *B.t.k.* (commercially available), which breaks down the gut lining of caterpillars.

Cutworms
　see Caterpillars

Deer
　Can decimate crops, woodlands and gardens; can kill saplings by rubbing their antlers on the trees, girdling the bark or snapping the trees in two; host ticks that carry Lyme disease.

What to do: many deterrents work for a while: encircle immature shrubs with tall, upright sticks; place dangling

Caterpillar on roses

Spittlebugs are unsightly but rarely cause damage.

soap bars around the garden; use noise makers or water spritzers to startle deer; mount flashy aluminum or moving devices throughout the garden.

Galls

Unusual swellings of plant tissues that may be caused by insects or diseases. Can affect leaves, buds, stems, flowers or fruit;

Deer-chewed cedars

often a specific gall affects a single genus or species.

What to do: cut galls out of plant and destroy them. Galls caused by insects usually contain the insect's eggs and juvenile stages; prevent such galls by controlling the insect before it lays eggs; otherwise try to remove and destroy infected tissue before young insects emerge. Insect galls are generally more unsightly than damaging to plants; galls caused by diseases often require destruction of plant. Don't place other plants susceptible to same disease in that location.

Gray Mold
see Blight

Grubs

Larvae of different beetles; white or gray body; head may be white, gray, brown or reddish; usually curled in C-shape; commonly found below soil level. Problematic in lawns; may feed on roots of perennials; plant wilts despite regular watering; may pull easily out of ground in severe cases.

Leaf miners

What to do: toss grubs onto a stone path, driveway, road or patio for birds to devour; apply parasitic nematodes or milky spore to infested soil (ask at your local garden center).

Leaf Miners

Tiny, stubby larvae of some butterflies and moths; may be yellow or green. Tunnel within leaves leaving winding trails; tunneled areas lighter in color than rest of leaf; unsightly rather than major health risk to plant.

What to do: remove debris from area in fall to destroy over-wintering sites; attract parasitic wasps with nectar plants such as yarrow or coriander; remove and destroy infected foliage; can sometimes squish larvae by hand within leaf.

Leaf Rollers
see Caterpillars

Leaf Skeletonizers
see Beetles

Leaf Spot

Two common types: one caused by bacteria and the other by fungi. Bacterial: small, brown or purple spots grow to encompass entire leaves; leaves may drop. Fungal: black, brown or yellow spots; leaves wither; e.g., scab, tar spot.

What to do: Bacterial: infection more severe; must remove entire plant. Fungal: remove and destroy infected plant parts; sterilize removal tools; avoid wetting foliage or touching wet foliage; remove and destroy debris at end of growing season.

Leafhoppers and Treehoppers

Small, wedge-shaped insects; can be green, brown, gray or multi-colored; jump around frantically when disturbed. Suck juice from plant leaves; cause distorted growth; carry diseases such as aster yellows.

What to do: encourage predators by planting nectar-producing species such as coriander. Wash insects off with strong spray of water; spray with insecticidal soap or neem oil according to package directions.

Maggots

Larvae of several species of flies (cabbage root maggots, carrot rust flies). Small, white or gray, worm-like. Tunnel into roots of a variety of plants, including many root vegetables. Stunt plants and disfigure roots; serious infestations can kill plants.

What to do: use floating row covers to prevent flies from laying eggs near roots. Apply parasitic nematodes to soil

Cabbage root maggots on radishes

around plants. Use an early crop of radishes as a trap crop. Pull them up and destroy them as soon as they become infested with maggots.

Mealybugs

Tiny, crawling insects related to aphids; appear to be covered with white fuzz or flour. Sucking damage stunts and stresses plant; excrete honeydew that promotes growth of sooty mold.

What to do: remove by hand from smaller plants; wash plant with soap and water or wipe with alcohol-soaked swabs; remove heavily infested leaves; encourage or introduce natural predators such as mealybug destroyer beetle and parasitic wasps; spray with insecticidal soap. Larvae of mealybug destroyer beetles look like very large mealybugs.

Mice

Burrow under mulch in winter, chewing plant roots, bark, tulip bulbs and many other underground goodies; even plants or roots stored in cool porches, garages or sheds are fair game.

Mealybugs

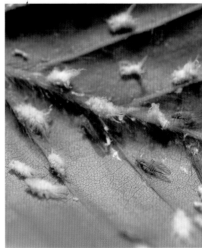

What to do: fine wire mesh can prevent mice from getting at your plants in winter, though the rodents are quite ingenious and may find their way through or around any barrier you erect; bulbs and lifted roots can be rolled in talcum powder, garlic powder or bulb protectant spray before storing or planting. Get a cat, or borrow your neighbor's, if you must.

Mildew

Two types, both caused by fungus, but with slightly different symptoms. Downy mildew: yellow spots on upper sides of leaves and downy fuzz on undersides; fuzz may be yellow, white or gray. Powdery mildew: white or gray, powdery coating on leaf surfaces that doesn't brush off.

What to do: choose resistant cultivars; space plants well; thin stems to encourage air circulation; tidy any debris in fall; remove and destroy infected parts.

Mites

Tiny, red, yellow or green, eight-legged relatives of spiders, e.g., bud mites, spider mites, spruce mites; almost invisible to naked eye; do not eat insects but may spin webs; usually found on undersides of plant leaves; may be fine webbing on leaves and stems or mites moving on leaf undersides. Suck juice out of leaves; leaves become discolored and speckled, then turn brown and shrivel up.

What to do: wash off with strong spray of water daily until all signs of infestation are gone; predatory mites are available through garden centers; spray plants with insecticidal soap.

Moles and Gophers

Burrow under the soil, tunneling throughout your property in search of

Powdery mildew on black-eyed Susan

insects, grubs and earthworms; tunnels can create runways for voles that will eat your plants from below ground.

What to do: castor oil (the primary ingredient in most repellents made to thwart moles and gophers) spilled down the mole's runway is effective and is available in granulated pellet form, too; noisemakers and predator urine are also useful; humane trapping is effective, as is having a cat or dog.

Mosaic

see Viruses

Neem Oil

The oil of the Indian neem tree, used in dilute form to kill bugs. Neem is a natural insecticide and will disable beneficial and harmful insects.

Sticky pheremone traps are useful for monitoring insect populations.

Nematodes

Tiny worms that give plants disease symptoms; one type infects foliage and stems; the other infects roots. Foliar: leaves have yellow spots that turn brown; leaves shrivel and wither; problem starts on lowest leaves and works up plant. Root-knot: plant is stunted and may wilt; yellow spots on leaves; roots have tiny bumps or knots.

What to do: mulch soil; add organic matter; clean up debris in fall; don't touch wet foliage of infected plants; add parasitic nematodes to soil; remove infected plants in extreme cases.

Rabbits

Can eat as much of your garden as deer and munch on the bark of trees and shrubs.

What to do: deterrents that work for deer usually keep rabbits away, as will humane trapping; having a cat or dog to patrol your garden may also be effective.

Raccoons

Are especially fond of fruit and some vegetables; can carry rabies and canine distemper; also eat grubs, insects and mice, so can sometimes be helpful to gardeners.

What to do: don't allow access to garbage or pet food; humane traps and relocation are best solutions; call your local SPCA or Humane Society to relocate individuals.

Rot

Several different fungi that affect different parts of plant, sometimes even killing it. Crown rot: affects base of plant, causing stems to blacken and fall over and leaves to yellow and wilt. Root rot: leaves turn yellow and plant wilts; digging up plant shows roots rotted away. White rot: a "watery decay fungus" that affects any part of plant; cell walls appear to break down, releasing fluids.

What to do: keep soil well drained; don't damage plant if you are digging around it; keep mulches away from plant base; destroy infected plant if whole plant is affected.

Rust

Fungi; pale spots on upper leaf surfaces; orange, fuzzy or dusty spots on leaf undersides; e.g., blister rust, hollyhock rust.

What to do: choose rust-resistant varieties and cultivars; avoid handling wet leaves; provide plant with good air circulation; clear up garden debris at end of growing season; remove and destroy infected plant parts.

Scab
see Leaf Spot

Scale Insects

Tiny, shelled insects that suck sap, weakening and possibly killing plant or making it vulnerable to other problems; once female scale insect has pierced plant with mouthpart, it is there for life; juvenile scale insects are called crawlers.

What to do: use alcohol-soaked swabs to wipe bugs off; spray plant with water to dislodge crawlers; prune out heavily infested branches; encourage natural predators and parasites; spray dormant oil in spring before bud break.

Slugs and Snails

Slugs lack shells; snails have a spiral shell; both have slimy, smooth skin; can be up to 8" long but are often much smaller; gray, green, black, beige, yellow or spotted. Leave large, ragged holes in leaves and silvery slime trails on and around plants.

What to do: attach strips of copper to wood around raised beds or smaller boards inserted around susceptible groups of plants (slugs and snails get shocked if they touch copper surfaces); pick off by hand in the evening and squish or drop in a can of soapy water; spread wood ash or diatomaceous earth (available in garden centers) around plants (it pierces their soft bodies and causes them to dehydrate); slug baits containing iron phosphate are not harmful to humans or animals and control slugs very well; if slugs damaged garden last season, begin controls as soon as new green shoots appear in spring.

Sooty Mold

Fungus; thin black film forms on leaf surfaces and reduces amount of light getting to leaf surfaces.

Snails (top) and slugs (center) can cause a lot of chewing damage to plants (bottom).

What to do: wipe mold off leaf surfaces; control aphids, mealybugs and whiteflies (honeydew left on leaves encourages mold).

Squirrels

Unearth and eat bulbs and corms, as well as flowers, fruits and vegetables; chew on sugar maples and hone their other teeth on almost everything else; raid birdfeeders and often eat the feeder itself; bury their food for later consumption, which can result in seeds germinating and plants springing up where you never wanted them.

What to do: cut heavy metal screening (hardware cloth) to fit around the plant stem; caging entire plants is effective if you don't mind your garden looking like a zoo; removing enticing food supplies is effective, but often impractical; trapping and moving is one option but usually results in other squirrels moving in to take their place.

Tar Spot
　　see Leaf Spot

Thrips
　　Tiny, slender, yellow, black or brown insects; narrow, fringed wings; difficult to see but may be visible if you disturb them by blowing gently on an infested flower. Suck juice out of plant cells, particularly in flowers and buds, causing mottled petals and leaves, dying buds, distorted and stunted growth.
　　What to do: remove and destroy infected plant parts; encourage native predatory insects with nectar plants such as yarrow or coriander; spray severe infestations with insecticidal soap or neem oil according to package directions.

Viruses
　　Include aster yellows, mosaic virus and ringspot virus. Plant may be stunted and leaves and flowers distorted, streaked or discolored.
　　What to do: viral diseases in plants cannot be treated. Control disease-spreading insects, such as aphids, leafhoppers and whiteflies; destroy infected plants.

Voles
　　Mouse-like creatures that damage plants at or just beneath the soil surface; mostly herbivorous, feeding on a variety of grasses, vegetables, herbaceous plants, bulbs (lilies are a favorite) and tubers; also eat bark and roots of trees, usually in fall or winter, and store seeds and other plant matter in underground chambers.
　　What to do: wire fences at least 12" high with a mesh size of ½" or less and buried 6–8" deep can help exclude voles from gardens. These fences can either stand alone or be attached to the bottom of an existing fence. A weed-free barrier

on the outside of the fence will increase its effectiveness. Burrow fumigants do not effectively control voles because the vole's burrow system is shallow and has many open holes. Electromagnetic or ultrasonic devices and flooding are also ineffective. When vole populations are not numerous or concentrated in a small area, trapping may be effective. Use enough traps to control the population: for a small garden, use at least 12 traps, and for larger areas, 50 or more may be needed. Again, a dog or cat is a deterrent. Do not use poisonous repellents or baits if your pets or children romp around the garden.

Weevils
    see Beetles

Whiteflies
    Tiny, white, moth-like flying insects that flutter up into the air when plant is disturbed; live on undersides of plant leaves. Suck juice out of leaves, causing yellowed leaves and weakened plants; leave behind sticky honeydew on leaves, encouraging sooty mold growth.
    What to do: destroy weeds where insects may live; attract native predatory beetles and parasitic wasps with nectar plants such as yarrow or coriander; spray severe cases with insecticidal soap; make a sticky flypaper-like trap by mounting a tin can on a stake, wrapping can with yellow paper and covering it with a clear plastic bag smeared with petroleum jelly (replace bag when it's covered in flies).

Wilt
    If watering doesn't help wilted plants, one of two wilt fungi may be to blame. *Fusarium* wilt: plant wilts; leaves turn yellow then die; symptoms generally appear first on one part of plant before spreading to other parts. *Verticillium* wilt: plant wilts; leaves curl up at edges;

leaves turn yellow then drop off; plant may die.
    What to do: both wilts are difficult to control; choose resistant plant varieties and cultivars; clean up debris at end of growing season; destroy infected plants; solarize (sterilize) soil before replanting (may help if entire bed of plants is lost to these fungi)—contact local garden center for assistance.

Woolly Adelgids
    see Aphids

Worms
    see Caterpillars, Nematodes

Compost Tea

2 lbs compost
5 gal water

Mix together and let sit for 4–7 days. Dilute mix with water until it resembles weak tea. Use during normal watering, or apply as a foliar spray to prevent or treat fungal diseases.

Homemade Insecticidal Soap

1 tsp mild dish detergent or pure soap (biodegradable options are available)
4 cups water

Mix in a clean spray bottle and spray the surfaces of your plants. Rinse well within an hour to avoid foliage discoloration.

About this Guide

The plants featured here are organized alphabetically by their most common familiar names. Additional common names appear as well. The scientific or botanical
name is always listed after the common name. Why learn the botanical names?
Several plants may share the same common name, and common names vary from
region to region. Only the botanical name identifies the specific plant anywhere in
the world.

Clearly indicated within each entry are the plant's height and spread ranges,
outstanding features and hardiness zone(s), if applicable. Each entry
gives clear instructions for starting and growing the plants,

and recommends many favorite selections. If height and spread ranges or hardiness zones are not given for every recommended plant, assume these ranges are the same as those provided in the Features section. Your local garden center will have any additional information about the plant and will help you make your plant selections.

Finally, the Problems and Pests section in each account deals with issues that afflict your garden plants from time to time. More information about common pests and diseases, including prevention and treatment, is given in the Problems and Pests section in the Introduction.

Amaranth

Amaranthus

Features: bushy, upright annual; red, purple, burgundy, gold or green plume-like flower clusters; edible young growth and seeds **Height:** 4–9' **Spread:** 12–36"

Amaranth provides one of the most complete sources of protein available in a grain. This drought-resistant plant is prolific, producing up to 10,000 seeds in a single flowerhead. Use the leaves and stems like spinach.

Combine amaranth with sunflowers for an impressive late-season display. The seed heads of both will be ready for harvesting around the same time.

Starting

Amaranth sprouts quickly when sown directly in the garden. Scatter seeds or plant in rows once all danger of frost has passed and the soil has warmed to at least 70° F.

Growing

Amaranth grows best in **full sun**. It adapts to most soil conditions but prefers a **fertile** soil. Spread a layer of compost to keep weeds down and improve the soil. Although it is drought tolerant, this plant grows best if the soil is kept fairly moist while it germinates.

Harvesting

The seeds usually ripen and drop in fall. There are several harvesting methods. Over a drop cloth, large bowl or bucket, shake or rub the seed heads between your hands—wear gloves, because the seed heads can be quite coarse. The seeds and plant bits are easy to separate; the plant bits are lighter and rise to the surface if you run your hands through the collected seeds while carefully allowing a fan to blow over them. The seeds are quite light, too, so the breeze should not be too strong. Leave the seeds to dry in a warm place before storing them in an airtight container.

Tips

Amaranth is very tall and makes a good screen. Attractive yellow, green and red foliage turn amaranth into a stunning summer landscape plant. In bloom, it resembles giant celosia, and it is related to that popular annual. Use the flowers in fresh or dried arrangements, but remember that cutting flowers will reduce your yield.

The grains can be added to soups and stews, cooked as a hot cereal or side dish, or ground into flour and used in pancakes, muffins and breads. They can even be popped, like corn, for snacking.

Recommended

A. hypochondriacus (amaranth, grain amaranth) is a tall annual that bears large, plume-like clusters of red, purple, gold or green flowers. It grows 4–9' tall and spreads up to 3'. **'Prince-of-Wales Feather,'** a red variety that tops out at 5' and spreads to 24", is used for both its leaves and seeds.

A. tricolor is a striking annual with variegated red, yellow and green leaves and insignificant flowers. **'Joseph's Coat'** resembles coleus. Thomas Jefferson liked it so much that he shipped seeds home to Virginia after discovering the plant in Europe. It grows 1–4' tall and up to 18" wide. Choose this variety for its edible leaves; sprinkle them raw in salads for extra color. Cultivars include **'Early Splendor'** and **'Molten Fountain.'**

Problems and Pests

Young plants look much like red-rooted pigweed, making weeding a challenge. If red-rooted pigweed is common in your garden, start your amaranth plants in peat pots, then transplant them directly into the garden to make weed identification easier.

Apples

Malus

Features: deciduous tree; red,
green or yellow fruit
Height: 8–20'
Spread: 10–30'

With careful
attention to the
chill factor, apples
can be grown
throughout
California. Choose
varieties for your
specific region
from local or
mail-order nurser-
ies. Standard trees
grow to 20' but can
be trimmed to 12'
or less for easier picking.
Dwarf and semi-dwarf trees are recommended for gardens. Apples are
delicious eaten out of hand, baked in pies and sliced in salads; their use
is only limited by your imagination. Branch out and try a variety not
carried in the grocery store. A single semi-dwarf tree may produce
hundreds of apples each season.

Starting

You can start an apple tree from seed—but choose a straight, bare-root or container tree instead and plant it about 18" deep, spreading the roots over a compost layer. Make sure the graft line is above ground.

Growing

Apples need **full sun** and **fertile, well-drained** soil. Consider planting two or more varieties for cross-pollination. Apples must be kept consistently **moist,** especially during the growing season. Dwarf and semi-dwarf trees work well in containers.

Harvesting

Apples ripen from July to November, depending whether they are early, mid-season or late varieties. Look for fruit in trees that are two to three years old.

Tips

Keep apple trees garden-size by trimming in late winter or spring. When space is limited, espalier the tree along a sunny wall or fence. If the fruit is small, try thinning early in the season. Add mulch around the base. For the best results, make sure your selection suits your geographic region.

Recommended

M. domestica is a tree of varying height with versatile, ripe fruit from July through November. Choose from an extensive selection based on region and chill hours.

Standard varieties grow 15–20' tall and spread 20–30'; semi-dwarf trees reach 10–15' tall and 15–20' wide; and dwarf varieties reach 8–10' tall and 10–12' wide.

Northern (above Santa Rosa): good options are **'Fuji,'** a well-known late bloomer with sweet, firm flesh; **'Golden Delicious,'** a late- to mid-season variety ideal for eating raw and cooking; and **'Honeycrisp,'** a disease-resistant, mid-season, sweet-tart red apple.

Northern Coastal (above San Luis Obispo): In addition to the northern recommendations, try **'Mutsu,'** a late greenish/yellow fruit that is great for desserts, and **'Jonagold,'** which produces flavorful large red-yellow apples late- to mid- season.

Sierra Nevada (above 2500'): try **'Empire,'** a mid-season cross between 'McIntosh' and 'Delicious,' which is crisp, juicy and tart; **'Haralson,'** whose juicy, somewhat tart fruit appears early to mid-season, and **'Liberty,'** a red, sweet-tart, late- to mid-season variety with disease resistance.

Central Valley: **'Dorsett Golden,'** an early bloomer that is great eaten raw or cooked; **'Granny Smith,'** a tart, old-time, mid-season favorite well-known for its use in pies; and **'Pink Lady,'** a sweet late variety good raw or cooked are good options.

Southern: Try low-chill varieties, including **'Anna,'** an early, crisp, sweet apple ideal for espaliering, and **'Gordon,'** a greenish-yellow, mid-season fruit with sweet-tart flavor. 'Fuji' and 'Granny Smith' are also suitable.

Problems and Pests

Diseases include scab, fire blight, powdery mildew, apple maggots and apple moth larvae. The best protection is to buy disease-resistant varieties. Cleaning up leaves and spraying with dormant oil will also help.

Apricots

Prunus

Features: deciduous tree; tasty stone fruit **Height:** 5–25' **Spread:** 5–25'

With their green and bronze leaves and pink or white blossoms, apricot trees beautify a garden while offering delicious fruit and shade. Early bloomers, these trees are not suitable for areas with late frosts. Southern gardeners should look for low-chill varieties. Prime apricot-growing regions like northern California and the San Joaquin Valley enjoy great harvests.

Starting

Look for straight bare-root or container trees that are at least one year old; fruit will not appear for another two or three years. Dig a hole at least 3 x 3' and mix compost and bonemeal in with the existing soil. Plant standard trees at least 20' from other trees; dwarfs need 8–12' of space.

Growing

Apricots thrive in **full sun** and **well-drained** soil. In cooler areas, place trees near a sunny wall. Water regularly, especially during fruiting.

Harvesting

Look for ripening fruit in June and July. Harvest fruit with a uniform color that gives slightly with pressure.

Tips

To improve overall fruit size, thin to three or four per cluster when apricots are about 1". Trim trees for easier picking.

Recommended

P. armenica is a fruiting tree widely grown in California for its beautiful, fragrant blossoms and tasty fruit. Choose a variety based on your geographic region and chill hours.

Standard varieties grow 15–25' tall and wide; semi-dwarf trees reach a height and spread of 12–18'; and dwarf varieties reach 12–18' tall and 5–10' wide.

Northern: **'Autumn Royal'** is an unusual fall ripener; **'Blenheim'** is a well-known California variety harvested early to mid-season; **'Floragold'** is a reliable early-producing semi-dwarf; and **'Moorpark'** has large, tasty fruit in mid-season.

Southern: Choose low-chill varieties, including **'Golden Amber,'** similar to 'Blenheim' with a month-long late-blooming period; **'Gold Kist,'** a delicious and prolific early bloomer; and **'Royalty,'** which bears large fruit earlier than most varieties.

Problems and Pests

Shot hole disease, a fungus that kills buds and discolors fruit, spreads during wet spring weather. Another fungus, brown rot blossom blight, is also found during wet weather. Fungicide application may help.

Packed with vitamin A and beta-carotene, apricots are delicious raw, cooked, canned and dried.

Artichokes
Globe Artichoke
Cynara

Features: bushy, tender perennial; spiny foliage; edible flower buds; purple, thistle-like flowers **Height:** 2–7' **Spread:** 4–6'

Native to the Mediterranean, these members of the thistle family do particularly well in cool coastal areas, where they're raised commercially. Try them in the San Francisco Bay area and in southern California, as well. Just make sure you've got horizontal space—a happy artichoke can spread to 6'.

Starting

In late winter or spring, plant container plants or divisions about 6" deep in well-drained soil. Keep the tops above ground level and water deeply and consistently. If starting from seed, try 'Imperial Star,' one of the only varieties that produces artichokes during the first season. Start seeds 8 to 12 weeks before the last frost, and set out transplants in warm soil after the danger of frost has passed.

Growing

Artichokes can take full sun along the coast but appreciate partial shade elsewhere. The soil should be **fertile, humus rich, moist** and **well drained**. During the growing season, water consistently and provide nitrogen-rich fertilizer.

After spring harvesting, cut the plant down to soil level and reduce or stop watering and fertilizing for several weeks. This forces dormancy during the hot summer. When you start watering again, you may get a second crop in fall.

To overwinter in colder areas, cover the plant with straw. Remove the straw in spring after the danger of frost has passed. Yield increases with age, so try to keep plants going.

Harvesting

Artichokes produce one large flower bud on the central stalk and many smaller flower buds on the side shoots. The flower

buds are rounded and made up of tightly packed scales. They are usually ready for harvest as the scales just begin to loosen. With a sharp knife, cut the flower bud from the plant about 4–6" below the bud's base. Cool weather crops, artichokes produce most reliably before the summer heat sets in. In cool summer

areas, artichokes produce September to May and sometimes all year.

Tips
Artichoke plants make dramatic additions to vegetable and ornamental gardens. A lovely silver-green, the plants sport long, arching leaves that make them look somewhat like ferns. And if you can resist eating the chokes, the huge purple flowers—up to 7" across—make stunning arrangements.

Recommended
C. scolymus forms a large clump of deeply lobed, pointy-tipped, gray-green leaves. It grows 2–7' tall and spreads 4–6'. In spring or sometimes fall, it bears large, scaled flower buds that open if not picked for eating. **'Green Globe'** is a popular cultivar because it is tasty and quick to mature and flower. **'Imperial Star'** is a heavy producer that's a good choice for short-season areas where frost or high heat is the norm. Grown as an annual, it produces artichokes only 90 days after transplanting.

Problems and Pests
Control slugs and snails by picking them off by hand or by using snail bait that contains iron phosphate. These products get rid of slugs and snails but are not toxic to pets. Hose off aphids.

Imagine how hungry someone must have been to risk fighting the thorns and thistles of the artichoke that very first time. Eating an artichoke is often a lesson in enjoying the journey as well as the destination—try the leaves dipped in butter and lemon as you work your way to the heart.

Asparagus

Asparagus

Features: perennial; edible spring shoots; ferny growth; small, white, summer flowers; decorative red fruit **Height:** 2–5' **Spread:** 2–4'

The large, ferny growth that asparagus develops comes as quite a surprise to first-time growers who may have seen only tidy bunches of spears at the grocery store. Asparagus is a member of the Lily family, and well-established plants can last a lifetime, producing tasty spears every spring.

Starting

Asparagus can be started from seed, or you can buy roots (also called crowns). A plant started from seed will be ready to start harvesting the third spring. A plant started from roots will be ready to begin harvesting the second spring.

Plant purchased roots in a well-prepared area. Work plenty of compost into the bed, then dig a trench or hole about 18" deep. Lay the roots 18–24" apart from each other and other plants. Cover the roots with 2–4" of soil and, as they sprout up, gradually cover them with more soil until the trench or hole is filled. Be careful not to cover the tips. Water and mulch well.

Plant seeds indoors in flats or peat pots about six to eight weeks before you will be planting them in the garden. Use larger pots if the seedlings get too big before you can move them outside. The first year, plant the seedlings at the soil level they are at in their pots. Keep them well watered and mulch with compost. The second summer, they can be planted in the same manner as roots, described above.

Growing

Asparagus grows well in **full sun** or **partial shade** with protection from the hot afternoon sun. The soil should be **fertile, humus rich, moist** and **well drained**. Apply a 4" layer of compost in spring and late summer. Weed regularly because this plant is most productive if it doesn't have a lot of competition from other plants.

Harvesting

As mentioned, asparagus spears that were started from roots are ready to be harvested two years after planting; spears started from seeds are ready in three years. Snap or cut the spears off at ground level for up to about four weeks in spring and early summer. When new spears are thinner than a pencil, you should stop harvesting and let the plants grow in. Add a new layer of compost to the soil when you have finished harvesting.

Tips

This hardy perennial plant is a welcome treat in spring and a beautiful addition to the back of a border.

Recommended

A. officinalis forms an airy mound of ferny growth. It grows 2–5' tall and spreads 2–4'. Small, white, summer flowers are followed by bright red berries, which can be collected for starting new plants. **'Jersey Giant,' 'Jersey Knight'** and **'Mary Washington'** are all reliable, delicious performers. For something different, try **'Purple Passion,'** said to be larger and sweeter than its green brethren.

Problems and Pests

Rust can be a problem, so choose resistant cultivars. Clean up debris in fall to discourage asparagus beetles. If you discover them during the growing season, handpick or spray them off with a water jet.

Avocados

Persea

Features: tropical evergreen tree; oval, green fruit encased in protective skin
Height: 8–12' **Spread:** 10–12'

Avocados are closely identified with the California lifestyle. Traditional varieties are quite large, growing 30–40' tall and wide, making them too large for most home gardens. The new, smaller cultivars discussed here allow home gardeners to enjoy these trees without sacrificing an abundance of yard. They grow about 12' and bear standard-size fruit.

Starting

Buy 5-gallon pots at a local or online nursery. If the temperature dips below 30° F, be prepared to cover your plants or move them inside. Protect them from hot, dry Santa Ana winds.

Growing

Place avocados in full **sun** to **partial shade**. In areas with very hot, harsh sun, protect young trees to avoid sunburn. These plants need **good drainage** and may get root rot if they don't get it. Add some sand to the planting hole to improve drainage. When transplanting, place the tree at the same level as it was in the nursery container. Avocados are delicate, so be careful handling the tree and the roots. During the growing season, provide occasional deep watering and let the basin dry between waterings.

Most dwarf avocados are self pollinating. Though considered evergreens, avocados drop their leaves. Keep the fallen leaves in place as mulch and add additional mulch so it spreads 2–3' from the trunk. Fertilize with an acidic citrus/avocado fertilizer four times a year.

Harvesting

Depending on the variety, avocados may ripen from May to January. Ripe fruit will also retain its quality if left on the tree.

Tips

Try a dwarf avocado in a container if your space is limited. Wheel it into the garage if frost threatens.

Recommended

P. americana is a tree with great-tasting fruit and large, leathery leaves. New varieties combine heavy production with small stature, making them ideal for home gardens. Growing them will make you popular with your neighbors. **'Holiday'** grows 10–12' and bears from August to January. Hardy to 30° F, it produces 15–30 ounce fruit from Labor Day to New Year's Day and retains its quality if left on the tree. **'Little Cado,'** also known as **'Wertz,'** grows to 8–10' with fruit that ripens from May to September.

Problems and Pests

Control root rot by mulching with a 6–12" layer of organic mulch or wood chips at least 6" from the tree.

Bananas

Musa

Features: herbaceous perennial; grows from underground rhizomes; white or orange flowers; distinctive, familiar fruit borne on stalks **Height:** 7–16' **Spread:** 8–10'

Attractive large, broad leaves make this a decorative landscape plant. The best choices for home gardens are dwarf trees that reach 7–16'. Tropical heat- and water-lovers, bananas do well along the coast.

Starting

Buy 5-gallon containers from local or online sources. Fruiting bananas do not cross-pollinate and have few, if any, seeds.

Growing

Bananas favor **sheltered** areas that are consistently **warm** and **sunny**. A space near a wall or fence is ideal. Plant in **sandy, acidic, well-drained** soil; drainage is very important. Water consistently during the summer growing season and don't let the plant dry out. During the rest of the year, water deeply but less frequently to avoid root rot. Fertilize every other month with a balanced fertilizer.

Some mature trees can handle freezing temperatures for short periods, but cover the plant if you expect prolonged periods below 28° F. Even if the top of the plant freezes, don't despair—bananas grow from the root system and you'll get fruit the following season. Keep temperature-damaged foliage in place as insulation until March. Stems die after fruiting; cut them off close to the ground. New stems emerge from the base.

Harvesting

Pick bananas individually when ripe or plump and green. Or cut off an entire bunch when green, hang it in a cool, dry place, and pick bananas from the top down as they ripen.

Tips

Bananas are attractive plants year-round that will give your garden tropical flair while offering fruit from late summer to fall. Look for those that produce dessert-type bananas, the kind found in supermarkets.

Recommended

M. acuminate cultivar **'Dwarf Cavendish'** is popular for home gardens. It produces sweet, dessert-type bananas and grows only 6–7' tall. Another small

variety, **'Dwarf Orinoco,'** is a heavy producer that tops out at 8'.

A little taller, the *M. manzano* variety **'Apple'** grows 14–16' and tastes like a cross between an apple and a sweet banana.

Problems and Pests

Keep aphids, scale and sooty mold away by controlling ants.

Basil

Ocimum

Features: bushy annual; fragrant, decorative leaves; white or light purple flowers
Height: 12–24" **Spread:** 12–18"

A member of the mint family, basil has a rich history in the cuisines of Iran, India and Asia. Versatile and easy to grow, basil now enjoys popularity throughout the world because it complements many different foods. The sweet, fragrant leaves of basil add a delicious, licorice-like flavor to salads, tomato-based dishes, soups, stews and more. Other basil flavors include cinnamon and lemon.

Starting

Basil is easy to start from seed. Start indoors about four weeks before the last frost date, or sow directly in sun-warmed soil once the danger of frost has passed. Press seeds into soil, then gently sift a little more soil over them. Keep soil moist. Seeds will germinate in about a week. Look for container-grown plants in mid-summer.

Growing

Basil grows best in a **warm, sheltered** location in **full sun**. The soil should be **fertile, moist** and **well drained**. Pinch the flowering tips regularly to encourage bushy growth and leaf production. Mulch the soil to retain water and to keep weeds down.

Harvesting

Pluck leaves or pinch back stem tips as needed. Basil is tastiest if used fresh, but it can also be dried or frozen.

Tips

Although basil grows best in a warm spot outdoors, it can be grown successfully indoors in a pot by a bright window, providing you with fresh leaves all year. Some of the purple-leaved varieties are very decorative and make fine borders.

Recommended

O. basilicum is one of the most popular culinary herbs. There are dozens of varieties, including ones with large or tiny, green or purple, smooth or ruffled leaves, as well as varied flavors including anise, cinnamon and lemon. **'Cinnamon'** basil smells like cinnamon and has a spicy-sweet taste. **'Green Globe'** forms a rounded mound of tiny leaves. **'Mammoth'** has huge leaves, up to 10" long and about half as wide. **'Purple Ruffles'** has dark purple leaves with frilly margins. **'Mrs. Burns'** is a citrus-scented heirloom disease-resistant lemon basil. Garnet-colored **'Red Rubin'** is one of the easiest basils to

O. basilicum

grow from seed, and **'Siam Queen'** is a cultivar of Thai basil with dark green foliage and dark purple flowers and stems

Problems and Pests

Fusarium wilt may afflict basil. Use *Bt* to keep caterpillars from chomping on your plants.

Basil makes a great companion for tomatoes because both require warm, moist growing conditions, and they are delicious when eaten together.

Bay Laurel

Laurus

Features: tender, evergreen shrub; aromatic foliage
Height: 1–40' **Spread:** 8"–40'

A Mediterranean native, bay laurel is easy to grow and makes an attractive houseplant. Bay leaves are commonly used in soups and stews.

Starting

Bay laurel can be started from seed, but germination may take up to six months. Plant the seeds in warm soil and keep the environment warm and moist but not wet, or the seeds will rot. It is simpler to purchase started plants, which are available from specialty growers and nurseries.

Growing

Bay laurel grows well in **full sun** or **partial shade**. A plant that will be moved indoors for winter should be grown in partial or light shade in summer. The soil should be **fertile, moist** and **well drained**. This plant has shallow roots and can dry out quickly in hot or windy weather. Mulch to reduce evaporation.

Bay laurel is not frost tolerant but may overwinter outdoors in a protected spot.

Harvesting

It may take a couple years before your bay laurel is leafy enough to be used on a regular basis. Pick fresh leaves as needed to use in cooking. Leaves can be dried and stored for later use, but this plant is evergreen, so you should be able to pick fresh leaves all year.

Tips

When planted in the ground, bay laurel can reach tree height—12–40' high and wide—making it useful as an aromatic hedge. As a shrub, it reaches 1–4' tall and 8–24" wide. If you simply want to cook with it, try it in a container to tame its growth. It makes an attractive addition to patios, decks and the steps of a staircase with other potted herbs, vegetables and flowers.

Recommended

L. nobilis is a bushy, evergreen shrub. **'Aureus'** is a cultivar with golden yellow foliage.

L. nobilis

Problems and Pests

Rare problems with scale insects and mealybugs are easy to solve by washing or rubbing smaller plants. Poor ventilation may lead to powdery mildew.

Bay laurel was used to make wreaths in ancient Greece.

Beans

Phaseolus

Features: bushy or twining, tender annual; attractive foliage; red, white or bicolored flowers; edible pods or seeds **Height:** 1–8' **Spread:** 12–18"

This incredibly diverse group of legumes includes beans eaten as pods, as immature seeds or as mature, dry seeds. Plants can be low and bushy or tall and twining. Plants are often prolific, and some are very attractive.

Starting

Beans are one of the easiest plants to grow from seed. They are large and easy to handle, and they sprout quickly in warm, moist soil. Plant them 4–8" apart, directly in the garden after the last frost date has passed and the soil has warmed up. Where winters are mild, plant in late winter or early spring.

Growing

Beans grow best in **full sun**, but they tolerate some light afternoon shade. They do best in **average, well-drained** soil. Plant in moist soil, then withhold water until seedlings pop up; keep soil consistently moist after that.

Bush beans support themselves, but climbing beans need a pole or trellis. Put a support structure in place at planting time to avoid disturbing young plants or damaging their roots.

Bush beans can become less productive and look unattractive as summer wears on. Pull them up and plant something else in their place, or plant them with companions that mature more slowly to fill in the space left by the faded bean plants.

Harvesting

The most important thing to remember when harvesting beans is to do so only when the foliage is dry. Touching wet foliage or plants encourages the spread of disease.

Different types of beans should be picked at different stages in their development. Green, runner, wax or snap beans are best picked when the pod is a good size but still young and tender. As they mature, they become stringy, woody and dry. Beans eaten as immature seeds should be picked when the pods are full and the seeds are fleshy and moist. Beans for drying are left to mature on

Legumes, like beans, are known for their ability to fix nitrogen from the air into the soil. They have a symbiotic relationship with bacteria, which attach to the roots as small nodules. The bacteria turn the nitrogen from the air into usable nitrogen for the plant; in return, the plant feeds and supports the bacteria. The bacteria are present in most soils and are also available for purchase as a soil inoculant. Some bean seeds are also pre-treated with the bacteria.

P. vulgaris (above), *P. lunatus* (below)

the plant. Once the plant begins to die back and before the seedpods open, cut the entire plant off at ground level and hang it upside down to finish drying. Remove the beans from their pods and store them in airtight containers.

Tips

Beans are very ornamental, with attractive leaves and plentiful flowers. Try growing climbing beans up fences, trellises, obelisks and poles to create a screen or feature planting. Use bush beans as low, temporary hedges or plant them in small groups in a border.

Recommended

P. coccineus (runner bean) is a vigorous climbing plant, with red, white or bicolored flowers. **'Scarlet Runner'** has bright red flowers and is one of the best and best-known cultivars. Eat the immature seeds with the pod when they are young and tender, or leave them to mature and dry the pink and purple spotted beans. Look for edible beans in 70 days and dry beans in 100 days.

P. lunatus (lima bean) may be climbing or a bush, depending on the cultivar. The beans are eaten as immature seeds and should be picked when the pods are plump but the seeds are still tender. They take 70 to 85 days to mature. **'Fordhook'** is a popular bush variety, and **'King of the Garden'** is a good climbing selection.

P. vulgaris (wax bean, green bean, bush bean, snap bean, dry bean) is probably the largest group of beans and includes bush beans and pole beans. Some are eaten immature in the pod, and others are grown to maturity and used as dry beans. Bush bean cultivars include yellow **'Eureka'** and **'Golden Roc d'Or'**; green, slim **'Jade'** and **'Rolande'**; or purple **'Purple Queen.'** Purple beans turn bright green when cooked. Bush

P. coccineus 'Scarlet Runner' (above & below)

beans take 50 to 60 days to mature. Pole beans, such as **'Blue Lake'** and **'Kentucky Blue,'** require 50 to 55 days to mature. Dry beans are usually bush plants and take about 100 days to mature. They include kidney, pinto and navy beans. Popular flageolet varieties like **'October Bean'** should be picked, shelled and cooked when green.

Problems and Pests

Problems with leaf spot, bacterial blight, rust, bean beetles and aphids can occur. Destroy diseased plant and do not compost them.

Climbing beans are popular among gardeners with limited space because they can maximize vertical gardening real estate.

Beets

Beta

Features: clump-forming biennial, grown as an annual; attractive, edible leaves; red, yellow or red-and-white-ringed, edible root **Height:** 8–18" **Spread:** 4–12"

Beets are versatile vegetables. While we often eat the plump, rounded or cylindrical roots, the tops are also edible and compare in flavor to spinach and Swiss chard. Beets and Swiss chard are closely related and are members of the genus *Beta*.

Starting

The corky, wrinkled seed of the beet is actually a dry fruit that contains several tiny seeds. Plant it directly in the garden around the last frost date. Even if you space the seeds 3–6" apart, you will probably have to thin a bit because several plants can sprout from each fruit. Go ahead and eat the thinnings. Beets are fairly quick to mature. Plant a second crop in mid-summer for a fall harvest. Where summers are hot, start in early spring so plants mature before the heat sets in.

Growing

Beets grow well in **full sun** or **partial shade** in cool weather. They favor **fertile, moist, well-drained** soil. Keep the soil evenly moist, and mulch lightly with compost to maintain moisture and improve soil texture.

Harvesting

Beets mature in 45 to 80 days, depending on the variety. Short-season beets are best for immediate eating and preserving, and long-season beets are the better choice for storing.

Pick beets as soon as they are big enough to eat. Tender when young, they can become woody as they mature.

When you want a few leaves, just pick them from an in-ground plant, selecting from a different location each time. Don't pull all the leaves off a beet.

Tips

Beets have attractive, red-veined, dark green foliage. They look good planted in small groups in a border and make interesting edging plants. For a lovely, edible display, try beets in large mixed containers.

Recommended

B. vulgaris forms a dense rosette of glossy, dark green leaves, often with deep red stems and veins. It grows 8–18"

tall and spreads 4–8". Many cultivars are available. **'Blankoma'** is a white beet. **'Chioggia'** is an heirloom cultivar that produces red-and-white-ringed roots. **'Cylindra'** has a long, cylindrical root. **'Detroit Dark Red'** is dark red and was developed from the heirloom **'Detroit.'** **'Golden Detroit'** has red skin and yellow flesh. **'Crosby's Egyptian'** and **'Red Sangria'** are good red, round cultivars. **'Touchstone Golden,'** with yellow skin and flesh, does not bleed, a factor that makes it a fine cooking and pickling choice.

Problems and Pests

Beets are generally problem free, but occasional trouble with scab, root maggots and flea beetles can occur.

Never fear if you get beet juice on your clothing; it won't stain. For centuries, dyers have tried unsuccessfully to find a fixative for beet juice. Chemists inform us that the red molecule in the beet is very large and doesn't adhere to other molecules, so a fixative is unlikely to be found.

Blueberries

Vaccinium

Features: deciduous shrub; small, bell-shaped, white or pink flowers; edible fruit; attractive habit; bright red fall color **Height:** 3"–5' **Spread:** 1–5'

These attractive bushes can be low and spreading or rounded and upright. The leaves turn a beautiful shade of red in fall. The plants are an admirable addition to any border, with the added asset of delicious summer fruit.

You can grow blueberries anywhere in California if you chose the proper variety for your region. Pay particular attention to the chill factor.

V. angustifolium

Starting

Look for bare-root or container-grown plants. In areas with cold winters, plant in spring; in warm-winter areas, plant in fall.

Growing

Blueberries grow well in **light shade to full sun**. They need **acidic, moist, well-drained** soil. Keep these shallow-rooted plants cool with a 3–4" mulch layer. For pollination, put in at least two plants.

Harvesting

Blueberries are ready for harvesting when they turn, not surprisingly, blue. Test one, and if it is sweet and tastes the way you expect, they are ready for harvest.

Tips

Extend blueberry season by planting early, mid- and late-season varieties. If your soil is alkaline, as it is in much of California, it may be easier to grow blueberries in a container full of acidic potting mix rather than amending the soil.

Recommended

V. corymbosum (highbush blueberry) is a bushy, upright, arching shrub with green leaves that turn red or yellow in fall. It grows 3–5' tall with an equal spread. Clusters of white or pink flowers at the ends of the branches in spring are followed by berries that ripen to bright blue in summer.

Up near the Oregon border, California gardeners have the perfect moist, cool-summer climate for growing traditional highbush blueberries like **'Blueray,'** a mid-season variety with large, flavorful berries;

'Chandler,' a mid-to-late season producer of large, sweet fruit; and **'Elliot,'** a late season choice with outstanding flavor.

Gardeners in the Sacramento area, the Central Valley and the south should seek out southern highbush varieties. These low-chill plants produce despite the warm summers. **'Cape Fear'** has a taste similar to that of wild blueberries. In some regions, these blueberries are evergreen, producing fruit year-round.

'**Misty**' reliably produces lots of great-tasting fruit. '**Reveille**' produces lots of tasty berries early in the season. '**Sunshine Blue**' is a self-fertilizing compact 3' grower with lots of tangy fruit.

Problems and Pests

Rare problems with caterpillars, rust, scale, powdery mildew and root rot can occur.

A handy way to preserve blueberries is to spread them on a cookie sheet and put them in the freezer. Once they are frozen, put them in an airtight bag and keep them in the freezer. The berries will be frozen individually, rather than in a solid block, making it easy to measure out just what you need for a single recipe or serving.

Borage

Borago

Features: bushy, bristly annual herb; edible, bristly leaves; edible, blue, purple or white summer flowers **Height:** 18–28" **Spread:** 18–24"

Borage leaves and flowers are both edible, making an interesting addition to salads. They have a very light, cucumber-like flavor. The flowers can also be frozen in ice cubes or used to decorate cakes and other desserts.

Starting

Sow seed directly in the garden in spring. This plant resents being transplanted thanks to a long taproot but recovers fairly quickly if moved when young.

Growing

Borage grows well in **full sun** or **partial shade**. It likes **average, light, well-drained** soil but adapts to most conditions and is a good drought-tolerant choice.

Borage is a vigorous self-seeder.

Harvesting

Pick borage leaves when they are young and fuzzy—they become bristly as they mature. Pick flowers any time after they open; they tend to change color from blue to pinkish mauve as they mature.

Tips

Borage makes an attractive addition to herb and vegetable gardens, as well as to flower beds and borders. The plant should be pinched back when young to encourage bushy growth; otherwise, it tends to flop over and develop a sprawling habit.

Recommended

B. officinalis is a bushy plant with bristly leaves and stems. It bears clusters of star-shaped, blue or purple flowers from mid-summer to fall. A white-flowered variety is available.

Problems and Pests

Rare outbreaks of powdery mildew and aphids are possible but don't seem to be detrimental to the plant.

Borage attracts bees, butterflies and other pollinators and beneficial insects to the garden.

Broccoli

Brassica

Features: bushy, upright annual; powdery, blue-green foliage; dense clusters of edible flowers **Height:** 12–36" **Spread:** 12–18"

Although usually thought of as a vegetable, broccoli could more accurately be called an edible flower. The large, dense flower clusters are generally eaten, though the stems and leaves are also edible. Broccoli is a member of the cabbage family.

Starting

Broccoli can be started from seed indoors or planted directly into the garden. Sow seeds indoors four to six weeks before the last frost date. Because seedlings can withstand limited cold, consider planting them outside two to four weeks before the last frost date. In warmer areas, set plants out in late summer, fall or winter.

Growing

Broccoli grows best in **full sun**. The soil should be **fertile, moist** and **well drained**. Broccoli performs best in cooler weather when nights are 60–70° F and days reach 80° F. Hot weather turns broccoli bitter and may cause bolting. Mix compost into the soil, and add a layer of mulch to keep the soil moist. Don't let this plant dry out excessively because it can delay flowering.

Harvesting

Broccoli forms a central head, and some varieties also produce side shoots. Pick the heads by cutting them cleanly from the plant with a sharp knife. If you leave them on the plant too long, bright yellow flowers will open.

Tips

Broccoli, with its blue-green foliage, is an interesting accent plant. Tuck it in groups of three or so into your borders and mixed beds for a striking contrast. This plant is susceptible to quite a few pests and diseases, and spacing it out rather than planting it in rows helps reduce the severity of potential problems.

Choosing a side-shoot-producing plant versus a main-head-only variety is a matter of personal preference. If you have a large family or plan to freeze some

florets, you may prefer a large-headed selection. If there are only a few people in the household, or you want to enjoy the broccoli for a longer time period without storing any, you may prefer the small-headed varieties that produce plenty of side shoots.

Recommended

B. oleracea var. botrytis is an upright plant with a stout, central, leafy stem. Flowers form at the top of the plant and sometimes from side shoots that emerge from just above each leaf. Plants grow 12–36" tall and spread 12–18". Maturity

dates vary from 45 to 100 days. **'Green Goliath'** sends out lots of side shoots during an extended three-week harvest rather than all at once. Popular in many areas of California, cold-tolerant **'Marathon'** produces in 97 days. **'Piracicaba'** has a looser head and many side shoots; it can handle warmer weather. **'Premium Crop'** is an All America Selections winner that matures early.

B. rapa ruvo (broccoli rabe), also known as rapini or Italian broccoli, is a related plant worth growing as well. It has loose florets, large leaves and stalks and a distinctive strong, peppery flavor. **'Super Rapini'** matures in 60 days.

Problems and Pests
Problems with cutworms, leaf miners, caterpillars, root maggots, cabbage white butterflies, white rust, downy mildew and powdery mildew can occur. Avoid planting broccoli in the same spot in successive years.

Cabbage white butterflies are common pests for all members of the Brassica *genus, and their tiny, green caterpillar larvae can be tough to spot in a head of broccoli. Break heads into pieces and soak them in salted water for 10 minutes before cooking. This kills the larvae and causes them to float to the surface.*

Brussels Sprouts

Brassica

Features: bushy, upright plant, grown as an annual; fat, edible buds sprout from leaf bases along the stem; blue-green foliage **Height:** 24" **Spread:** 18"

Love them or hate them, Brussels sprouts are at the very least a garden curiosity. Developing a stout central stem, the sprouts form on the stem at the base of each leaf. The display is unique and eye-catching.

Starting

Buy small transplants or start seeds indoors about six weeks before you expect to put them in the garden. Sow seeds in peat pots to make it easier to transfer seedlings to the garden. Cold-region gardeners should plant in spring for fall harvest. In warmer areas, plant in late summer or fall and harvest in spring.

Growing

Brussels sprouts grow well in **full sun**. The soil should be **fertile, moist** and **well drained**. Brussels sprouts need a fairly long growing season to produce sprouts of any appreciable size, so plant them they as early as possible. Regular moisture encourages quick maturation; keep the soil well mulched. Once you see sprouts forming, remove some stem leaves to give sprouts more growing room.

Harvesting

Pick sprouts as soon as they are large and plump, but before they begin to open. A light frost can improve their flavor. The entire plant can be pulled up, and if you remove the roots, leaves and top of the plant, the sprouts can be stored on the stem in a cool place for up to four weeks. Be watchful—they go bad quickly.

Nutrient-rich and fiber-packed, Brussels sprouts deserve a more prominent place on our plates. When picked after a light frost, steamed so that they are cooked just through to the center and served with butter, they are delicious. You can also roast them in the oven to bring out their sweetness.

Brussels sprouts are categorized into early-, mid- and late-season varieties. If you want a regular harvest, choose plants from each category. If you consider them a late-fall treat, look for mid- or late-season varieties.

Tips

Brussels sprouts create a leafy backdrop for your flowering annuals and perennials.

Recommended

B. oleracea var. *gemnifera* is an upright plant that develops a single leafy stem. Sprouts form at the base of each leaf along the stem. The leaves are blue-green, often with white mid-ribs and stems. Many varieties offer ongoing harvest over several weeks. **'Oliver,'** an early season choice, provides sprouts in 90 days. Other popular cultivars include

'Bubbles,' 'Long Island Improved' and 'Tasty Nuggets.' Try mid-season 'United' along the coast. If you want something unusual, consider 'Rubine,' a purple-red heirloom.

Problems and Pests

Problems with cutworms, leaf miners, caterpillars, root maggots, aphids, cabbage white butterfly larvae, white rust, downy mildew and powdery mildew can occur.

To avoid overcooking Brussels sprouts, cut an X in the stem about one-quarter of the way through each sprout to help the inside cook at the same rate as the outside.

Cabbage

Brassica

Features: biennial grown as an annual; dense, round, red, purple, blue-green or green, leafy clumps; smooth or crinkled leaves **Height:** 18–24" **Spread:** 12–18"

Cabbages are easy to grow, and they create a dense, leafy, often color-ful display. They come in three forms: green with smooth leaves, green with very crinkled leaves and red or purple with (usually) smooth leaves.

Starting

Start seeds indoors about six weeks before you plan to transplant them outdoors. You can also direct sow them into the garden around the last frost date as long as the soil has warmed up a bit. Where winters are mild, plant in fall or winter.

Growing

Cabbages grow best in **full sun** but will grow in partial shade in hot areas. They prefer cool growing conditions and benefit from mulch to retain moisture during hot weather. The soil should be **fertile, moist** and **well drained**.

Harvesting

The leaves of young plants can be eaten. When a good-sized head has developed, cut it cleanly from the plant. Smaller heads often appear once the main head has been cut. Cabbages that take a long time to mature (three to four months from transplant) generally store better than types that mature quickly (seven to eight weeks).

Tips

Choose a variety of cabbages because the different colors, textures and maturing times create a more interesting display in rows or mixed borders.

Recommended

B. oleracea **var.** *capitata* is a low, leafy rosette that develops a dense head. Leaves may be green, blue-green, red or purple and smooth or crinkled. It matures in 60 to 140 days, depending on the variety. Some popular smooth-leaved, green varieties are early producers, including **'Copenhagen Market,'** **'Early Jersey Wakefield,'** **'Famosa,'** **'Golden Acre,'** **'Point One'** and **'Tendersweet.'** Mid- to late-season varieties include **'Greenback,'** **'Late Flat Dutch'** and **'Savor.'** Popular crinkled or savoy types are **'Savoy Ace'** and **'Savoy King.'**

For distinctive red cabbages, consider **'Cabbage Salad Delight'** and **'Ruby Perfection.'**

Problems and Pests

Problems with cutworms, leaf miners, caterpillars, root maggots, aphids, cabbage white butterfly larvae, white rust, downy mildew and powdery mildew can occur.

*Don't forget that all members of the cabbage genus (*Brassica*) are susceptible to many of the same pests and diseases. Don't plant them in the same spot two years in a row, particularly if you've had disease problems in that area.*

Calendula
Pot Marigold, English Marigold
Calendula

Features: hardy annual; yellow, orange, cream, gold or apricot, edible flowers; long blooming period **Height:** 10–24" **Spread:** 8–20"

Bright and charming, calendula is a Mediterranean native that produces attractive, colorful flowers in summer and fall.

Starting

Calendula grows easily from seed. Sprinkle the seeds where you want them to grow (they don't like to be transplanted), and cover them lightly with soil. They will sprout within a week. Young plants are available at nurseries.

Growing

Calendula does equally well in **full sun** or **partial shade**. The soil should be of **average fertility** and **well drained**. Calendula likes cool weather and can withstand a moderate frost.

Deadhead the plant to prolong blooming and keep it looking neat. If your plant fades in the summer heat, cut it back to 4–6" above the ground to encourage new growth. A fading plant can also be pulled up and new seeds planted. Both methods provide a good fall display.

Harvesting

Pick the flowers as needed for fresh use, or dry the petals for later.

Tips

This informal plant looks attractive in borders and mixed in among vegetables or other plants. It can also be used in mixed planters and container gardens. Calendula is a cold-hardy annual and often continues flowering, even through a layer of snow, until the ground freezes completely.

Recommended

C. officinalis is a vigorous, tough, upright plant that grows 12–24" tall and spreads 10–20". It bears single or double, daisy-like flowers in a wide range of yellow and orange shades. **'Bon Bon'** is a dwarf plant that grows 10–12" tall and bears flowers in shades of yellow, orange and apricot. Other dwarfs include **'Dwarf Gem'** and **'Fiesta.'** **'Pacific Beauty'** is an heirloom cultivar with large, brightly colored flowers. It grows 18–24" tall. **'Radio'** is a tall variety with quilled petals.

Problems and Pests

Calendula is usually trouble free. It continues to perform well even when afflicted with rare problems such as aphids, whiteflies, smut, powdery mildew and fungal leaf spot.

Calendula flowers are popular kitchen herbs that can be added to stews for color or to salads for flavor.

Caraway

Carum

Features: hardy biennial; feathery, light green foliage; clusters of tiny, white flowers; edible seeds **Height:** 8–24" **Spread:** 12"

Used for more than 5000 years, caraway is a tasty addition to savory and sweet dishes. The seeds are used in sauerkraut, stews, rye bread, pies and coleslaw.

Starting

Caraway can be started from seed and should be planted where you want it to grow, because it can bolt quickly when the roots are disturbed.

Growing

Caraway grows best in **full sun** but tolerates some shade. The soil should be **fertile, loose** and **well drained**. This plant is biennial and generally doesn't bloom until the second year. It is a vigorous self-seeder.

Harvesting

Cut the ripe seed heads from the plants, and place them in a paper bag. Loosely tie the bag closed, and hang it in a dry location. Once the seeds are dry, they can be stored in an airtight jar. The seed heads are ripe when the seedpods just begin to open.

Tips

Caraway doesn't have a very strong presence in the garden, but it can be planted in groups with more decorative plants where its ferny foliage and pretty white flowers add a delicate, airy touch.

Recommended

C. carvi is a delicate-looking, upright biennial with ferny foliage. In the second summer after sowing, white flowers are borne in flat-topped clusters.

Problems and Pests

Caraway rarely suffers from any pests or problems.

Plant caraway near cabbage to attract predatory insects and to remind to you to add caraway seed to your cabbage as it cooks. Caraway helps reduce the cooking odor and flatulence associated with cabbage.

Carrots

Daucus

Features: biennial grown as an annual; feathery foliage; edible root **Height:** 8–18"
Spread: 2–4"

There is nothing quite as satisfying as pulling a perfect, crisp, sweet carrot out of the garden and crunching away as you go about your work. With all of the different sizes and colors available, carrots are a fun crop to grow with children.

Starting

Carrots can be sown directly in the garden once the last frost date has passed and the soil has warmed up. The seeds are very tiny and can be difficult to plant evenly. Mix the tiny seeds with sand before you sow them to spread the seeds evenly and reduce the need for thinning. You can also purchase seeds that have been coated with clay to make them easier to handle. Cover very lightly with sand or compost when planting because the seeds can't sprout through too much soil. Keep the seedbed moist to encourage even germination.

Growing

Carrots grow best in **full sun**. The soil should be **average to fertile, well drained** and **deeply prepared**. Because you are growing carrots for the root, you need to be sure that the soil is loose and free of rocks to a depth of 8–12". This gives carrots plenty of space to develop and makes them easier to pull up when they are ready for eating. If your soil is very rocky or shallow, you may wish to plant carrots in raised beds to provide deeper, looser soil, or grow shorter varieties.

To keep carrots for a long time, store them in a cold, frost-free place in containers of moistened sand.

Spacing carrots is a gradual process. As the carrots develop, pull a few of the more crowded ones out, leaving room for the others to fill in. This thinning process will give you an indication of how well they are developing and when they will be ready to harvest. The root can be eaten at all stages of development.

Harvesting

Never judge carrots by their greens. Big, bushy tops are no indication that carrots are ready for picking. As the roots develop, you will often see the carrot top at or just above soil level, which is a better indication of development.

In loose soil, pull carrots with a good grip on the greens. Harvesting in heavy soil may require a small garden fork.

Tips

Carrots make an excellent ornamental grouping or edging plant. The feathery foliage provides an attractive background for flowers and plants with ornamental foliage.

Recommended

D. carota var. *sativus* forms a bushy mound of feathery foliage. It matures in 50 to 75 days. The edible roots may be orange, red, yellow, white or purple. They come in a variety of shapes, from long and slender to short and round. The type you choose will depend on the flavor you like, how long you need to store them and how suitable your soil is. **'Baby Babette'** is a tasty baby variety. **'Danvers Half-Long'** develops tasty, deep orange roots that grow well in clay soil and are suitable for overwintering. **'Ithaca'** is a reliable grower that produces 7" carrots under less-than-perfect conditions. **'Lady Finger,' 'Short 'n Sweet'** and **'Thumbelina'** are all miniatures. 'Thumbelina' develops small, 2" round roots, which grow well in poor soil or containers. **'Napoli'** is a sweet carrot that matures early. **'Yaya'** grows to about 6" and holds well in the ground. For non-traditional colors, try **'Purple Haze,'** a purple-skinned looker with orange flesh, and pure red **'Nutri-red.'** **'Rainbow'** produces roots in white, yellow and several shades of orange.

Problems and Pests

Carrot rust flies and root maggots can sometimes be troublesome.

Many supermarket varieties sold as "baby" carrots are whittled-to-size adults. By growing your own, you'll get to enjoy the flavor of true young carrots.

Cauliflower

Brassica

Features: annual; white, purple, green, yellow or orange, edible flowerheads
Height: 18–24" **Spread:** 18"

If you think of pure white heads when you think of cauliflower, you may be surprised by all the different colors available through seed vendors. Orange, purple, green and the classic white are all readily available.

Starting

Cauliflower can be sown directly in the garden around the last frost date, or you can start them indoors about four weeks before you plan to set them outdoors. In areas where winters are mild, plant in fall or winter.

Growing

Cauliflower grows best in **full sun**. The soil should be **fertile, moist** and **well drained**. This plant favors cool, humid weather. In warm areas, search out heat-resistant varieties and avoid planting for summer harvest.

Cauliflower must have a rich soil that stays evenly moist, or heads may form poorly, if at all. Mix plenty of compost into the soil, and mulch with compost to help keep the soil moist.

Harvesting

Unlike broccoli, cauliflower does not develop secondary heads once the main one is cut. Cut the head cleanly from the plant when it is mature. You can then compost the plant.

Tips

White cauliflower may turn yellow or greenish unless some of the leaves are tied over the head to shade it from the sun. Use elastic or string to tie the leaves when you first notice the color changing.

Recommended

B. oleracea var. *botrytis* is leafy and upright with dense, edible flower clusters in the center of the plant. Most selections take 70 to 85 days to mature, though some mature in as few as 45 days. Popular white-headed cultivars include **'Snowball,'** the heat-tolerant **'Snow King'** and early-season **'Early Dawn.'** **'Concert'** sports leaves that are

particularly suitable as shields from the sun. Attention-grabbing purple varieties include **'Graffiti,'** with good wrapping leaves, and **'Violetta di Sicilia,'** an Italian heirloom that produces side shoots after the main head is cut. **'Verdant'** and **'Veronica'** (another heat-tolerant selection) are green-headed cultivars, and 'Veronica' produces florets that form pointed, tapering peaks. **'Cheddar'** is an orange-headed cultivar that contains 25 times the amount of Vitamin A as white cauliflower. If you simply can't decide, try **'Multicolor Blend'** with orange, purple and green heads.

Problems and Pests

Cutworms, leaf miners, caterpillars, root maggots, aphids, cabbage white butterfly larvae, white rust, downy mildew and powdery mildew can occur. Like its family member broccoli, cauliflower attracts green caterpillar larvae. Break heads into pieces and soak them in salted water for 10 or so minutes before cooking. This kills the larvae and causes them to float to the surface.

Purple cauliflower generally turns green when cooked.

Celery & Celeriac

Apium

Features: biennial grown as an annual; bushy habit; edible stems; bright green
leaves **Height:** 18" **Spread:** 10"

If you think celery isn't worth growing in the home garden, think again.
Crisp, flavorful ribs of garden-fresh celery are far superior to what is
available in the grocery store. Celeriac, also known as celery root, is used
raw in salads or cooked in soups and stews.

Starting

Celery and celeriac thrive in warmth but not heat. In cool regions, start seed indoors at least eight weeks and up to 12 weeks before you plan to transplant it outdoors. Be patient; seed can take up to three weeks to germinate. Be sure to keep the planting medium moist, but not soggy. Avoid planting out until the last frost date has passed and the soil has warmed. In warmer areas, set plants out in fall. Mulch plants to conserve moisture.

Celery and celeriac seeds are tiny; look for coated, pelleted varieties for easy handling. Celery is also available in nursery packs. Celeriac is less commonly grown and is best purchased as seed.

Growing

Celery and celeriac grow best in **full sun** but enjoy light or afternoon shade in hot weather. The soil should be **fertile, humus rich, moist** and **well drained**. Allowing the soil to dry out too much

Cold nights can cause celery to flower, leaving the stalks inedible, or at least unpalatable.

will give you a poor quality, bad-tasting vegetable.

In late summer, you can mound soil around the celery stalks or wrap them in newspaper to shade them from the sun and to encourage the development of the familiar pale green or blanched stems. Unblanched stalks have a stronger flavor that some people prefer.

Celeriac is a large, edible root with the same cultivation requirements as celery.

Harvesting

Celery stalks can be harvested one or two at a time from each plant. If you are blanching the stems before picking them, they will be ready for harvesting two or three weeks after the stalks are covered. A light touch of frost can sweeten the flavor.

Celeriac should be harvested before the first fall frost. Pull plants up, remove the leaves and store the knobby roots the same way you would beets or carrots, in a cold, frost-free location in a container of moistened sand.

Tips

Celery and celeriac have light green leaves that create a very bushy backdrop for flowering plants with less attractive, spindly growth.

Recommended

A. graveolens var. *dulce* (celery) is a bushy, upright plant with attractive, light to bright green foliage. It matures

in 100 to 120 days. Self-blanching **'Golden Boy'** is prized for its tender leaves. **'Tango'** has tender, less fibrous stalks and withstands heat. The heirloom **'Red Stalk'** stays red when cooked.

A. graveolens var. *rapaceum* (celeriac) forms a bushy, bright green plant that develops a thick knobby, bulbous root. It matures in 100 to 120 days. **'Brilliant,' 'Mentor'** and **'Ibis'** are popular cultivars.

Problems and Pests

Problems with fungal blight, mosaic virus, *fusarium* yellows, bacterial and fungal rot, leaf spot and caterpillars can occur.

Blanching is a gardening technique usually used on bitter-tasting vegetables. Partially or completely depriving the plant of light sweetens the flavor. Although many devices have been developed to make blanching easier, a good mound of soil or mulch will do the job just fine.

Chamomile

Matricaria

Features: bushy annual; fragrant, feathery foliage; daisy-like flowers
Height: 12–24" **Spread:** 6–8"

Chamomile's pretty, flavorful flowers make a perfect after-dinner tea. The flowers can also be dried and stored so that you can enjoy chamomile tea through the winter months. This delicate, airy plant is useful for filling in garden spaces wherever it is planted.

Starting

Start seeds about four weeks early indoors or sow directly in the garden once the last frost date has passed. In warm areas, sow in late fall for spring harvest.

Growing

Chamomile grows well in **full sun** or **partial shade**. The soil should be of **average fertility, sandy** and **well drained**. Chamomile self-seeds freely if you don't pick all the flowers.

Harvesting

As the flowers mature, the petals fall off and the centers swell as the seeds start to develop. At this point, the flowers can be picked and used fresh or dried for tea.

Tips

Chamomile is an attractive plant to use along the edge of a pathway or bed where the fragrance will be released when the foliage is brushed, bruised or crushed. The flowers attract beneficial insects, so you may also want to plant a few here and there among your other plants.

Recommended

M. recutita (German chamomile) is an upright annual with soft, finely divided, fern-like foliage and bears small, daisy-like flowers in summer. It grows 12–24" tall and spreads 6–8".

Problems and Pests

Chamomile rarely suffers from any problems.

Chamomile tea is a relaxing beverage to have before bed or after a meal to help settle the stomach.

Chard

Swiss Chard

Beta

Features: biennial grown as an annual; glossy, green, purple, red or bronze, edible foliage; green, white, yellow, orange, pink, red or purple stems and veins
Height: 8–18" **Spread:** 12"

A type of beet, chard is one of the garden's most useful vegetables. The wide range of colors makes it a valuable ornamental addition to beds, borders and even container gardens.

'Bright Lights'

Starting

The corky, wrinkled seed of chard is actually a dry fruit that contains several tiny seeds. Plant the dry fruit directly in the garden around the last frost date. Where summers are mild, plant in fall. Even if you space the seeds 3–6" apart, you will probably have to thin out a bit because several plants can sprout from each fruit. Nursery plants are easy to find in spring.

Growing

Chard grows well in **full sun** or **partial shade**. It grows best in cool weather. The soil should be **fertile, moist** and **well drained**. Mulch lightly with compost to maintain moisture and to improve the soil.

Harvesting

Chard matures quickly, and a few leaves can be plucked from each plant every week or so. You can generally start picking leaves about a month after the seed sprouts.

Tips

Chard has very decorative foliage. Glossy green leaves complemented by

brightly colored stems and veins in shades of red, pink, white, yellow or orange make a colorful statement in borders. The bushy, clumping habit looks lovely in mixed container plantings.

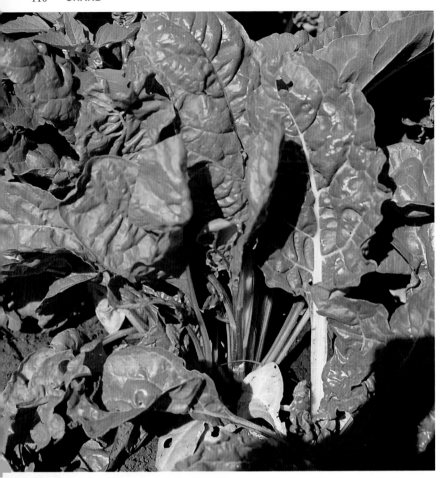

Recommended

B. vulgaris subsp. ***cicla*** forms a clump of glossy, green, purple, red or bronze leaves that are often deeply crinkled or savoyed. Stems and veins may be pale green, white, yellow, orange, pink, red or purple. Plants grow 8–18" tall and spread about 12". Popular cultivars include **'Fordhook Giant,'** a white-stemmed heirloom; **'Pot of Gold,'** with bright yellow stems; **'Perpetual,'** a non-bolting, heat-resistant cultivar with pale green stems; **'Bright Lights,'** with a combination of red, orange, yellow or white stems; **'Rainbow'** ('Five Color

Silverbeet'), which adds pink to the mix; **'Scarlet Charlotte,'** with bright red stems; sweet, mild **'Neon Glow'** with gold and magenta stems; and **'Silverado,'** with creamy white stems.

Problems and Pests

Rare problems with downy mildew, powdery mildew, leaf miners, aphids, caterpillars and root rot can occur.

If you find that chard fades during the heat of summer, plant a second crop in fall for fresh leaves in spring.

Chives

Allium

Features: spiky habit, narrow green foliage; mauve, pink or white flowers **Height:** 8–24" **Spread:** 12" or more

The delicate onion flavor of chives is best enjoyed fresh. Mix chives into dips, or sprinkle them on salads and baked potatoes. The blooms are striking in the garden and in salads and herbal vinegars.

A. schoenoprasum

Starting

Chives can be started indoors four to six weeks before the last frost date or planted directly in the garden. They also can be purchased as plants.

Growing

Chives grow well in **full sun** or **partial shade**. The soil should be **fertile, moist** and **well drained**, but chives adapt to most soil conditions. Plants self-seed freely in good growing conditions. The youngest leaves are the most tender and flavorful, so cut plants back to encourage new growth if flavor diminishes.

Harvesting

Chives can be snipped off with scissors all spring, summer and fall, as needed. Flowers are usually used just after they open, and the individual flowers in the cluster are broken apart for use.

Tips

Include decorative chives in a mixed or herbaceous border and let them naturalize. In an herb garden, give them plenty of space for self-seeding.

Recommended

A. schoenoprasum (chives) forms a clump of bright green, cylindrical leaves. Clusters of pinkish purple flowers are produced in early and mid-summer. Varieties with white or pink flowers are also available.

A. tuberosum (garlic chives) forms a clump of long, narrow, flat, dark green leaves. Clusters of white flowers are borne all summer. The young leaves have a distinctive garlic flavor. This species self-seeds more readily than other types.

Problems and Pests

Chives rarely have any problems.

Chives are said to increase appetite and encourage good digestion.

Citrus

Citrus, Fortunella

Features: fruiting tree; fragrant blossoms **Height:** 8–22' **Spread:** 6–20'

Citrus varieties grown widely in California include lemons, limes, oranges, grapefruit, pummelo and kumquat. Beautiful, fragrant and productive, they fit perfectly in the garden. The small stature of dwarf varieties makes them ideal for containers.

Starting

Look for straight bare-root or container grown trees from nurseries, home centers or online retailers. Position the tree in a frost- and wind-free location in a sunny area. Use reflected heat from garden walls to your advantage. Because citrus varies in its cultural requirements, make sure to purchase plants suitable for your region.

Growing

Citrus needs a warm spot in **full sun** with **well-drained** soil. Carefully remove the tree from the pot and plant it with the crown slightly above ground level. Keep the soil moist but don't let water stand. Water deeply. Mulch with 2–4" of compost. Where winters are cold and temperatures linger near freezing, try easily movable citrus in wheeled containers and transfer them to shelter.

Harvesting

Harvest times depend on the variety. Although citrus fruits most heavily in fall and winter, some types do so year-round. Citrus ripens on the tree.

Tips

All citrus require heat and sun, and they vary in their ability to withstand cold and frost. Many are available as compact dwarfs. Lemons and limes are good choices for cool summer areas because they need the least heat to ripen. If you live in an area where heat is consistently intense, try grapefruit. Hot summers and cold winters? Consider kumquats.

Recommended

Standard trees reach 18–22' tall and 10–20' wide; dwarf trees grow 8–10' tall and 6–10' wide.

C. aurantifolia (lime) includes seedless 'Bearss,' a good choice for cool areas, and sweet, thin-skinned 'Mexican Sweet Lime.'

C. grandis 'Chandler' (pummelo) has large, pink-fleshed fruit.

C. limon 'Eureka' (lemon) produces tart fruit year-round.

C. x meyeri 'Improved Meyer' (Meyer lemon) is sweeter and has thinner skin than Eureka lemon; the variegated, pink-fleshed 'Pink Lemonade' is a beautiful landscape plant with white and green leaves.

C. paradisi (grapefruit) includes the popular 'Oro Blanco' and red-fleshed 'Star Ruby' and 'Ruby Red.'

C. reticulate var. *mandarin* (mandarin orange) is also known as tangerine. Hardy 'Owari Satsuma' begins to ripen in October, but you can still pick this easy-to-peel variety in February; sweet 'California Honey' fruits from January through April.

C. sinensis 'Washington' (navel orange) is sweet and seedless, perfect for eating right off the tree; 'Lane Late' fruits in summer and extends the season with an orange suitable for fruit or juice; 'Valencia,' the popular juice orange, has fruit that lasts on the tree.

F. crassifolia 'Meiwa' (kumquat) is sweet and juicy. Kumquats seem to defy categorization. They were considered part of the citrus family until 1915, when they were transferred to the genus *Fortunella*. Modern plant experts favor their return to the citrus label.

Problems and Pests

Keep ants off citrus to forestall other pest problems.

Coriander & Cilantro

Coriandrum

Features: airy, delicate habit; fern-like foliage; flat, pinkish white flowers in summer
Height: 18–24" **Spread:** 8–18"

Coriander is a multi-purpose herb. The leaves, called cilantro, are used in salads, salsas and soups. The seeds, called coriander, are used in cakes, pies, chutneys, stews and marmalades. The flavor of each is quite distinct.

Starting
Coriander can be started from seed four to six weeks before the last frost date or sown directly in the garden. Started plants can also be purchased from nurseries, garden centers or herb specialists. Several small sowings two weeks apart will ensure a steady supply of leaves.

Growing
Coriander prefers **full sun** but benefits from afternoon shade during the heat of summer. Heat may cause bolting. The soil should be **fertile, light** and **well drained**. This Mediterranean native dislikes humid conditions and does best during a dry summer.

Harvesting
Harvest leaves as needed. Seeds can be harvested as they ripen. To collect seeds, spread out a large sheet and shake the seed heads over it.

Tips
Coriander has pungent leaves that release scent when brushed. The plant is a delight to behold when in flower. Add a plant here and there throughout your borders, both for the visual appeal and to attract beneficial insects.

Recommended
C. sativum is an annual herb that forms a clump of lacy basal foliage and produces large, loose clusters of tiny, pink-white flowers. The seeds ripen in late summer and fall.

Problems and Pests
This plant rarely suffers from any problems.

Coriander is one of the best plants for attracting predatory insects to your garden.

Corn

Zea

Features: annual grass; broad, strap-shaped leaves; tassel-like flowers
Height: 4–8' **Spread:** 12–24"

Corn is believed to have originated in South America. Widely grown
by Native peoples in both North and South America, corn is one of
the "Three Sisters" of Native gardens. Corn, beans and squash were
grown together as companions. The beans fixed nitrogen in the soil
and used the corn for climbing support. The large leaves of squash
shaded the soil and kept weeds to a minimum.

Starting

Start seed directly in the garden two weeks after the last frost date; seed will rot if the soil is too cold. Depending on the variety, corn can take from 75 to 110 days to mature. If your growing season is short or the soil is slow to warm, you may prefer to start your corn four to six weeks early in peat pots and transplant it to the garden after the last frost date.

Growing

Corn grows best in **full sun**. The soil should be **fertile, moist** and **well drained**. Water deeply. As the plant develops, you can mound more soil around its base; the stem will develop roots in this soil, and the plant will be stronger and less likely to blow over in a strong wind. Look for early-, mid- and late-season varieties to keep corn on your table all season long.

Harvesting

Corn is ready to pick when the silks start to turn brown and the kernels are plump. Check for readiness by popping

There are ornamental varieties of corn available; some, such as 'Fiesta' and 'Seneca Indian,' have colorful kernels on the cobs; others, such as 'Harlequin' and 'Variegata,' have foliage striped in red, green and white or creamy white, respectively.

a kernel. Watery liquid means you're too early; no liquid means you're too late. If you get milky liquid, pick the corn and enjoy it. Heirloom varieties should be picked and used as quickly as possible because they begin to turn starchy as soon as they are picked. Newer genetically modified selections have increased sweetness and stay sweet after picking.

Tips

Corn is wind pollinated, so plants need to be fairly close together for pollination to occur. Planting in groups improves pollination rates. Corn is an architectural grass that looks similar to some of the upright ornamental grasses, such as miscanthus. Plant it in groups of five to nine in your beds and borders for the most attractive effect.

Recommended

Z. mays is a sturdy, upright grass that has bright green leaves with undulating edges. Plants grow 4–8' tall and spread 12–24". **Var. *rugosa*** (sweet corn) matures in 65 to 80 days and falls into

Avoid growing both popcorn and sweet corn, or keep them well separated. They can cross-pollinate, which can make both inedible.

several sweetness categories. These gauge both how sweet the corn is and how quickly the sugar turns to starch once the corn is picked. Some of the sweeter corns are less tolerant of cold soils. Kernels can be white or yellow, or cobs may have a combination of both colors. The sugar-enhanced **'Bodacious'** is ready mid-season. A Japanese variety, **'Mirai,'** is very sweet and matures in 71 days. **'Silver Princess'** is a disease-resistant hybrid that ripens early. If you prefer heirloom varieties that have not been modified, try **'Golden Bantam'** with sweet, yellow 6–7" ears and **'Stowell's Evergreen,'** a white sweet corn introduced in 1848. **Var. *praecox*** (popcorn) matures in 100 to 110 days and has shorter cobs with yellow, white or red, hard kernels.

Problems and Pests

Corn earworms, aphids, caterpillars, downy mildew, rust, smut and fungal leaf spots can affect corn.

Cucumbers

Cucumis

Features: trailing or climbing, annual vine; decorative leaves; yellow flowers; edible fruit **Height:** 12", when climbing **Spread:** 4–8', when trailing

Whether you have a passion for pickling or think a salad just isn't a salad without the cool crispness of cucumber, you have a wide range of cucumbers to choose from that grow well in California gardens. And there's no doubt about it—homegrown cucumbers are far superior to anything you can buy at your local grocer.

Starting

Cucumbers can be started indoors about four weeks before the last frost date or sown directly into the garden once the last frost date has passed and the soil has warmed up. If you start them inside, use peat pots to avoid root damage.

Growing

Cucumbers grow well in **full sun** or **light shade**. The soil should be **fertile, moist** and **well drained**. Consistent moisture is most important during germination and fruit production. Go vertical by tying vines onto a trellis using soft ties such as strips of old nylons.

Harvesting

Harvest timing depends on the cucumber type. Pick pickling cucumbers when they are young and small. Harvest slicing cukes when they are small if you want to pickle them; let them mature for other uses. Pick long, slender Oriental cucumbers when they are mature.

Plants keep producing provided the fruit doesn't stay too long on the vine. Pick cucumbers as soon as they are a good size for eating. The more you pick, the more the plants will produce.

Tips

Cucumbers are versatile. They can be left to wind their way through other plants or grown up trellises or other supports. The mound-forming varieties make attractive additions to a container garden.

Recommended

C. sativus is a trailing, annual vine with coarse-textured leaves and bristly stems. It matures in 45 to 60 days. Popular slicing and salad cucumbers include the long, slender **'English Telegraph'** and **'Sweet Success.'** A disease-resistant dwarf, **'Bush Slicer'** is great in salads and in containers. **'Spacemaster'** is a high-yielding, space-saving cultivar. **'Green Fingers,'** a Baby Persian variety with 3–5" fruit, resists disease. Popular cultivars of pickling cucumbers include the disease-tolerant, semi-bush **'Cross Country'** and the prolific **'Pickalot.'**

Problems and Pests

Problems with powdery mildew, downy mildew, mosaic virus, white flies, aphids, cucumber beetles, bacterial wilt, leaf spot, scab and ring spot can occur.

Wondering about the round, yellow cucumber in the photo? 'Lemon' is a heritage variety with a crisp texture and mild flavor; it's great in salads. The vines are trailing, and because the fruit is not too heavy, they are ideal for growing up a low trellis.

Dill

Anethum

Features: feathery, edible foliage; yellow, summer flowers; edible seeds
Height: 2–5' **Spread:** 12" or more

Dill is majestic and beautiful in any garden setting. Its leaves and seeds are probably best known for their use as pickling herbs, though they have a wide variety of other culinary uses.

Starting

Dill can be sown directly in the garden around the last frost date. Make several small sowings every couple of weeks to ensure a steady supply of leaves.

Growing

Dill grows best in **full sun** in a **sheltered** location out of strong winds. The soil should be of **poor to average fertility, moist** and **well drained**. Sow seeds in place. Don't grow dill near fennel because the two plants will cross-pollinate, and the seeds of both plants will lose their distinct flavors.

Harvesting

Pick the leaves as needed throughout summer and dry them for use in winter. Harvest the seeds by shaking the seed heads over a sheet once they ripen in late summer or fall.

Tips

With its feathery leaves, dill is an attractive addition to a mixed bed or border. Include it in a vegetable garden or in any sunny location. Dill also attracts butterflies and beneficial insects to the garden.

Recommended

A. graveolens is an annual herb that forms a clump of feathery foliage. Clusters of yellow flowers are borne at the tops of sturdy stems.

Problems and Pests

Dill rarely suffers from any problems.

Eggplant
Solanum

Features: frost-tender perennial commonly grown as annual; large, attractive, lobed leaves; purple flowers; versatile globular, egg-shaped or elongated fruit
Height: 2–4' **Spread:** 2–3'

Thought to be a native of India, eggplant is a beautiful, productive member of the nightshade family, which also includes tomatoes. Despite its heritage, standard eggplant—the large, dark purple globe found in the grocery store— has come to be known as Italian eggplant, and it also comes in white, rose, green and striped versions. Asian egg- plant is long and slender.

Starting

Buy container-grown plants or start from seed indoors six to eight weeks before setting plants outside. Place plants in warm, moist, well-drained soil after any danger of frost has passed.

Growing

Eggplant grows best in **full sun** with consistent warmth (daytime temperatures between 70 and 85° F) over a two to three month period. Water deeply and regularly and mulch. Eggplant does best in **fertile, loamy, well-drained** soil.

Harvesting

Harvest fruit when it is bright, shiny and firm. Otherwise, it will turn bitter. Pick Italian eggplant when it is 4–6" in diameter and 6–9" inches long; pick Asian fruit when it is 4–6" inches long. Cut eggplant from the woody stalk using a knife or scissors rather than pulling. Keep harvesting to produce more fruit.

Tips

Where long, hot summers aren't the norm, consider growing eggplant near a sunny wall where it can bask in reflected heat, or put it in a movable container to catch the sun's rays wherever they land.

Recommended

S. melongena is a heat-loving perennial grown as an annual with globe-shaped or cylindrical, elongated fruit and purple, star-shaped flowers. Standard, or Italian, varieties with large, purple fruit include **'Black Beauty,' 'Early Bird'** and **'Dusky.'** The beautiful heirloom **'Rosa Bianca'** bears fruit with white and pink skin and white flesh on 2'-high plants. Fruit is 5–7" long and 4–6" wide.

Asian types include **'Ichiban,'** an easy-to-grow choice with 4–6" slender, dark purple fruit, and the lovely lavender white **'Asian Bride'** with 8" fruit and

white flesh. A white variety, **'Gretel'** won the All American Selections Award and produces shiny 3–4" fruit on compact plants.

Problems and Pests

Eggplant occasionally suffers from *fusarium* wilt. Control aphids to prevent other insect problems.

Fennel

Foeniculum

Features: short-lived perennial or annual; attractive, fragrant foliage; yellow, late-summer flowers; edible seeds **Height:** 2–6' **Spread:** 12–24"

All parts of fennel are edible and have a distinctive, licorice-like fragrance and flavor. The seeds are commonly used in baked goods or to make a tea that is good for settling the stomach. Florence fennel produces a large, swollen base that is eaten raw in salads, cooked in soups and stews or roasted like other root vegetables.

Starting
Start seeds directly in the garden after the danger of frost has passed.

Growing
Fennel grows best in **full sun**. The soil should be **average to fertile**, **moist** and **well drained**. Avoid planting fennel near dill or coriander to avoid the possibility of cross-pollination, which reduces seed production and makes the seed flavor of each less distinct. Fennel easily self-sows.

Harvesting
Harvest fennel leaves as needed for fresh use. When the seeds are ripe, in late summer or fall, harvest them by shaking the seed heads over a sheet. Dry the seeds before storing. Harvest Florence fennel as soon as the bulbous base becomes swollen. Pull plants up as needed, and harvest any left in the ground before the first fall frost.

Tips
Fennel is a lovely addition to a mixed bed or border. The flowers attract pollinators and predatory insects to the garden.

Recommended
F. vulgare is a short-lived perennial that forms clumps of loose, feathery foliage. Clusters of small, yellow flowers are borne in late summer, followed by seeds that ripen in fall. **Var. *azoricum*** (Florence fennel, anise) is a biennial that forms a large, edible bulb at the plant base.

Problems and Pests
Fennel rarely suffers from any problems.

Bronze fennel is attractive as well as delicious. The feathery bronze foliage adds a distinctive touch to flower beds and borders.

Fiddlehead Ferns

Matteuccia

Features: perennial fern; attractive foliage; edible, tender shoots **Height:** 3–5'
Spread: 12–36"

These popular, classic ferns are revered for their delicious, emerging
spring fronds and their stately, vase-shaped habit. Fiddlehead ferns
are at their best in cold winter regions.

M. struthiopteris

Starting

Crowns can be purchased and planted out in spring. Plants are sometimes also available in summer. They are often sold as ornamental plants in the perennial department of your local garden center or nursery.

Growing

Fiddlehead ferns prefer **light or partial shade** and tolerate full shade, or full sun if the soil stays moist. The soil should be **average to fertile, humus rich, neutral to acidic** and **moist**. Leaves may scorch if the soil is not moist enough. These fronds are aggressive spreaders that reproduce by spores; give them a large area to spread so you'll have plenty of fronds to harvest. This fern is not a good choice for regions with mild winters.

Harvesting

Let plants become established for a few years before you begin harvesting. Pick new fronds in spring as they begin to uncurl, and be sure to pick no more than half the fronds from each plant.

Tips

These ferns appreciate a moist woodland garden and are often found growing wild alongside woodland streams and creeks. Useful in shaded borders, these plants are quick to spread.

Recommended

M. struthiopteris (*M. pensylvanica*) forms a circular cluster of slightly arching, feathery fronds. Stiff, brown, fertile fronds covered in reproductive spores stick up in the center of the cluster in late summer and persist through winter. They are popular choices for dried arrangements.

Problems and Pests

These ferns rarely suffer from any problems.

The tightly coiled, new spring fronds taste delicious when lightly steamed and served with butter. Remove the bitter, reddish brown, papery coating before steaming.

Figs
Ficus

Features: frost-tender deciduous fruit tree; sweet fruit; bright green leaves
Height: 15–30' **Spread:** 6'

Native to Asia and the Mediterranean, figs are beautiful garden trees that also do well in containers. Some varieties need heat; others thrive in cooler temperatures. Choose a variety that suits your region.

F. carica 'Violette de Bordeaux'

Starting
Choose a container-grown tree and plant it in regular soil.

Growing
Figs like **sun**, regular water and **fertile, humus-rich, well-drained** soil. They have shallow roots, making them difficult garden bed partners, and they can be invasive, which is another reason to plant them in a container. Most garden varieties are self-pollinating. In colder areas, espalier against a south-facing wall or protect the trees during frost. Even if they do freeze, figs will usually produce new shoots the following year.

Harvesting
Let figs ripen on the tree. A ripe fig is slightly soft and will detach easily. Keep figs in the refrigerator for up to three days. Figs are also delicious dried. In areas where frost is not a problem, figs often bear in spring and fall.

Tips
Beware of fruit drop near patios and pools. Figs can be messy. These are tall trees, growing 15–30' but can be trimmed to 6'; or choose a dwarf variety or espalier in home gardens.

Recommended
F. carica is a deciduous tree with sweet, sticky fruit and an attractive, low branching habit. Where summers are cool, try **'Improved Brown Turkey,'** a producer of large, brown-skinned figs well suited for home gardens; cool-region favorite **'Desert King,'** with green skin and red flesh; **'Excel,'** a cold-hardy fig with yellow fruit that does well in containers; and **'Osborn Prolific,'** a very sweet, brown-skinned fig at home on the northern coast. In warmer regions, also consider semi-dwarf **'Black Jack,'** with large purple fruit and red flesh; delicious **'Violette de Bordeaux,'** a dwarf with dark purple fruit and strawberry-colored flesh; coastal and coastal valley favorite **'Genoa,'** with yellow green skin and pink flesh; and **'Black Mission,'** a heavy-bearing, purple-black variety brought to California by early missionaries.

Problems and Pests
Figs are subject to mosaic virus and gopher attacks.

Flax

Linum

Features: upright annual; blue flowers; edible seeds **Height:** 12–36"
Spread: 8–18"

Flaxseed has long been added to baked muffins, breads and cereals. It is now being hailed for its fantastic health-improving potential and is an excellent source of omega-3 fatty acids.

L. usitatissimum (above & below)

Starting
Start seed directly in the garden in spring around the last frost date.

Growing
Flax grows best in **full sun**. The soil should be of **average fertility, light, humus rich** and **well drained**.

Harvesting
When they are ripe, harvest the seeds by rubbing the seed heads between your hands over a sheet or bucket. Dry the seeds completely before storing them in a cool, dry place.

Tips
Flax is a beautiful plant that many gardeners grow for its ornamental appeal alone. Each flower lasts only one day and is replaced by another each day once blooming begins.

Recommended
L. usitatissimum forms clumps with leafy, upright stems that wave at the slightest breeze. The blue, summer flowers are followed by chestnut brown, pale brown or golden yellow seeds in late summer or fall.

Problems and Pests
Problems with rot, rust, wilt, slugs, snails and aphids can occur.

This species is not used exclusively as a food source; the stems of some cultivars are processed to produce linen. Linseed oil also comes from the seeds of flax.

Garlic

Allium

Features: perennial bulb; narrow, strap-like leaves; white summer flowers
Height: 6–24" **Spread:** 8"

Garlic is not the most ornamental plant, but the light green leaves make a good groundcover and repel several common garden pests.

Starting

Garlic is generally grown from sets (cloves) that can be started in fall or spring. Also try planting cloves from the grocery store. Plant them with the pointed end up. Where winters are mild, plant in fall for a spring crop.

Growing

Garlic grows best in **full sun**. The soil should be **fertile, moist** and **well drained**.

Harvesting

This plant can be dug up in fall once the leaves have yellowed and died back. Lift gently with a garden fork to avoid cracking the bulbs. Softneck garlic can be stored for a longer time than hardneck varieties, but it is not as hardy.

Tips

Although the flowers are quite attractive and often intriguing, they should be removed so the plant devotes all its energy to producing bulbs rather than seeds. Garlic takes up little space and can be tucked into any spare spot in your garden.

Recommended

A. sativum var. *ophioscordon* (hard-neck garlic) has a stiff central stem around which the cloves develop.

A. sativum var. *sativum* (softneck garlic) develops more cloves but has no stiff stem. The soft leaves are often used to braid garlic bulbs together for storage.

Problems and Pests

A few rot problems can occur, but this plant is generally trouble free.

Grapes

Vitis

Features: deciduous vine; edible fruit; attractive heart-shaped leaves **Height:** 10'
Spread: 10'

Grape vines provide shade and ornamental value as well as fruit that is suitable for snacking, preserving and drinking. Choose a variety well suited to your climate and be prepared to trim and train it for the best results. Fast growers, grapes make lovely landscape plants. Look for fruit in shades of yellow, green, red and purple. One vine can cover 50 to 100 square feet, depending on the variety.

Starting

Choose bare-root plants from a local nursery or online source and plant them when they are dormant—in winter in mild climates or about three weeks before the last frost elsewhere. Soak roots for two to three hours before planting. Set the plant in the ground at the same level as it was in the nursery pot. Be ready to provide strong support with an arbor, espalier or other structure.

Growing

Grapes require **full sun** and prefer **fertile, well-drained** soil. Deep growers, they require root space of at least 3–4'. Work compost into the soil to provide the best growing environment. Give them 1" of water per week until established. Many varieties are self-pollinating. Though the vines grow quickly, abundant fruit production may take several years.

Harvesting

Grapes ripen from August through October. Choose from early, middle and late varieties. Taste the fruit to test for ripeness.

Tips

Grapes draped over an attractive arbor or trellis or espaliered on a sunny wall make a distinctive and delicious statement in the garden. Pruning techniques vary and involve trimming spurs or canes during dormancy. Fruit grows on year-old wood. A single grape vine can cover up to 100 square feet. Prune to suit your location.

Recommended

V. labrusca (fox grape) is the American variety and is more cold tolerant, withstanding temperatures down to 0° F. For cool regions, consider seedless **'Canadice,'** a red early ripener; **'Interlaken,'** a seedless green/yellow hybrid with sweet flavor; and early, red-skinned **'Reliance.'** In warmer regions, try the well-known **'Concord,'** which has dark blue seeded fruit with rich flavor; spicy, seedless **'Himrod,'** a white early ripener; and **'Niagara,'** a mid-season green/yellow favorite good for eating or beverages.

V. vinifera (European grape) prefers more warmth and a longer growing season. In cooler areas, good choices include early mid-season **'Black Monukka Seedless'** for snacking or drying and **'Perlette Seedless,'** a pale yellow early ripener. In warmer regions, try early **'Crimson Seedless'** for great flavor; **'Delight,'** a yellow-green variety good for eating and drying for raisins; and well-known **'Thompson Seedless,'** a mid-season favorite for hot, dry regions.

Problems and Pests

Make sure grapes get seven to eight hours of sun each day to avoid powdery mildew. European varieties are the most susceptible. Pierce's disease can kill the vine and is spread by insects.

V. labrusca 'Concord'

Guavas

Feijoa, Psidium

Features: frost-tender, multi-branched, evergreen shrub or tree; pink or white, fragrant flowers; sweet, 2–4" fruit; smooth bark flakes off to reveal attractive underlayer
Height: to 30' **Spread:** to 25'

Guavas are selective about their heat requirements. They like an average temperature of above 60° F but will perish with intense heat.

Starting

Start from seed or plant purchased seedlings. Place them outside in a container or in the ground when the soil is warm.

Growing

Guavas like **full sun** in cooler areas but require **partial shade** where temperatures are higher. They will grow in many types of soil as long as it is **well drained**. Water deeply but allow the soil to dry between irrigation cycles. Once established, these plants are drought-tolerant.

While many are self-pollinating, fruiting is more reliable if another guava is nearby. If the temperature drops below freezing, the leaves may fall—but your guava could survive. Look for new shoots the following year. Fruit is borne on new growth.

Guava can grow to 30' tall and can spread 25', but most home garden varieties are trimmed to 6–8' shrubs.

Harvesting

Guavas fruit year-round in mild areas and in spring elsewhere. Ripe guavas have a distinctive fragrance. Allow guavas to ripen on the tree for the best flavor, or let the fruit drop to the ground. Otherwise, pick it when it is nearly mature and place it in a bag with an apple or banana to ripen it further. The fruit is soft and bruises easily.

Tips

To promote fruiting, encourage honeybees to visit your guavas by planting flowering herbs like oregano and thyme nearby.

Recommended

F. sellowiana (pineapple guava) is a tropical evergreen tree or shrub that can reach 25' but is trimmed to 8–10' for gardens. Though related to traditional guavas, it originated in Brazil from a different genus (montypic). It features fragrant, edible summer flowers and small seeds; the fruit has a distinct flavor reminiscent of pineapple. Pineapple guava is hardy to 12° F. Cultivars include **'Nazemetz,'** whose fruit does not turn brown after cutting; **'Improved Coolidge,'** which has large, October-ripening fruit and is good in cool coastal areas; and **'Moore,'** a large, reliable, mid-season fruit producer.

P. cattleianum (strawberry guava) grows to 25' feet but is usually trimmed to an 8–10' shrub. More cold hardy than traditional guavas, it produces round, red-skinned fruit that is 1½–2" in diameter with hard seeds and tastes something like a strawberry. It is more resistant to insect problems than *P. guajava*.

P. guajava is a tropical, deciduous fruit tree with oval-shaped fruit. In some varieties, the skin and seeds are edible. The fruit of **'Benjamin'** ripens around Thanksgiving and is large and sweet; **'Mexican Cream'** has fruit with yellow skin and white flesh; sweet **'White Indonesian'** bears several times each year.

Problems and Pests

Mealybugs, scale and white fly can bother guava.

Guavas are high in vitamins A and C and are full of fiber. They're delicious eaten fresh or juiced.

F. sellowiana

Horseradish

Armoracia

Features: clump-forming perennial; pungent, edible root; glossy, green, creased leaves **Height:** 24–36" **Spread:** 18" or more

Horseradish is a plant that is too often relegated to a neglected back corner of the garden. Despite its rampant ability to spread, it has beautiful foliage that makes it a prime candidate for perennial and mixed borders.

Starting

Plants can be purchased or grown from a division or a piece of root. A new plant will generally grow from even a small piece of root.

Growing

Horseradish grows well in **full sun**. The soil should be **fertile, moist** and **well drained**, but the plant adapts to most conditions.

Harvesting

When foliage dies back in fall, dig up some roots to use fresh or in preserves, relishes and pickles. The roots have the strongest flavor in fall, but they can be harvested any time once the plant is well established.

Tips

Horseradish is a vigorous plant that spreads to form a sizeable clump. It is fairly adaptable and can be in an out-of-the-way area, but it deserves a better spot because of its glossy, creased foliage.

Recommended

A. rusticana forms a large, spreading clump of large, puckered, dark green leaves. Plants grow up to 36" tall and spread 18" or more.

Problems and Pests

Generally problem free, horseradish can occasionally suffer from powdery mildew, downy mildew, fungal leaf spot or root rot.

Horseradish sauce is a popular garnish for roasted meats, roast beef in particular.

Kale, Collards & Mustard Greens

Brassica

Features: tender biennial; bronze, purple, blue-green or glossy green, sometimes deeply wrinkled, decorative, edible leaves **Height:** 18–24" **Spread:** 18–24"

These nutrient-packed leafy cabbage and broccoli siblings are some of the most decorative members of this family. A southern staple, collards grow quite happily in California and make a welcome change from cabbage and kale. Mustards are most often eaten when quite young and lend a spicy flavor to stir-fries and salads. Robust, versatile kale shows up in many international dishes, such as the Irish side dish colcannon, a kale-potato combo, and Portuguese caldo verde soup, in which kale mixes with spicy sausage, potatoes, broth and olive oil.

Starting

Sow seeds directly in the garden or set out transplants. These cool-season vegetables do well planted in fall in warmer areas; where summers are cool, plant in spring for an early-summer harvest. A light frost won't harm them and might even make them sweeter. Cover the young plants if nighttime temperatures reach 15° F or lower. You may wish to make several successive plantings of mustard because the leaves have the best flavor when they are young and tender.

Growing

These plants do well in **full sun** or **partial shade** in hot inland areas. The soil should be **fertile, moist** and **well drained**. Mustard in particular should not be allowed to dry out, or the leaves may develop a bitter flavor.

Harvesting

Unlike their cousins broccoli and cauliflower, these plants do not form a head but instead send up a loose collection of large leaves. Once plants are established, you can start harvesting leaves as needed. Pick a few from the outer parts of each plant.

Tips

Edible leaves appear quickly, so you don't have to wait very long to enjoy your harvest. These plants make a striking addition to beds and borders, where the foliage creates a good complement and backdrop for plants with brightly colored flowers. Full of vitamins A and C, the leaves make snappy additions to stir fries and soups

Recommended

B. oleracea subsp. *acephala* (kale, collards) and *B. juncea* subsp. *rugosa* (mustard) form large clumps of ruffled, creased or wrinkled leaves in shades of green, blue-green, bronze and purple. Kale varieties include heirloom **'Lacinato'** (also known as **'Dinosaur'** or **'Tuscan Black'**), a vigorous plant with nicely flavored large leaves, and **'Nero de Toscano,'** with attractive bluish leaves. Dwarf varieties suitable for containers include **'Dwarf Blue Curled'** and **'Dwarf Siberian.'** Both do well in warm inland valleys. **'Champion'** collards keep their fresh flavor longer than some other varieties. **'Giant Red'** and **'Mizouna'** are popular mustard selections.

Problems and Pests

Problems with cutworms, leaf miners, caterpillars, root maggots, cabbage white butterfly larvae, white rust, downy mildew and powdery mildew can occur. Kale, collards and mustard greens are less troubled by pests and disease than other members of the family.

Kohlrabi

Brassica

Features: biennial grown as an annual; pale silvery or gray-green foliage; edible, bulbous stem base **Height:** 12" **Spread:** 12"

The tender, swollen stem base of kohlrabi has a very strange appearance. The leaf bases become stretched as the bulb forms, and new leaves continue to sprout from the top of the rounded bulb. The name comes from the German *kohl* ("cabbage") and "rabe" ("turnip") because the plant is in the cabbage family yet forms an edible above-ground turnip-like bulb.

Starting

Sow seed directly in the garden about two weeks after the last frost date. In areas with warm winters, sow again in fall. This plant matures quite quickly, so make several small sowings one or two weeks apart to have a continuous supply of tender, young kohlrabi.

Growing

Kohlrabi grows best in **full sun**. The soil should be **fertile, moist** and **well drained**, though plants adapt to most moist soils.

Harvesting

Keep a close eye on your kohlrabi because the bulb can quickly become tough and woody if left too long before harvesting. The bulb is generally well rounded and 2–4" in diameter when ready for harvesting. Pull up the entire plant and cut just below the bulb, then cut off the leaves and stems and compost them or use to mulch the bed.

Tips

Low and bushy with white or purple bulbs, kohlrabi makes an interesting edging plant for beds and borders and can be included in container gardens, particularly those where plants are changed regularly.

Recommended

B. oleracea subsp. *gongylodes* forms a low, bushy clump of blue-green foliage. As the plant matures, the stem just above ground level swells and becomes rounded. This part is the edible portion. White varieties include **'Early White Vienna'** and **'Grand Duke.'** **'Early Purple Vienna'** is an interesting purple alternative.

Problems and Pests

Problems with cutworms, leaf miners, caterpillars, root maggots, cabbage white butterfly larvae, white rust, downy mildew and powdery mildew can occur.

Encourage good growth by keeping the soil moist, and harvest the bulbs quickly once they form.

Leeks

Allium

Features: biennial often grown as an annual; narrow, upright growth with long, arching, strap-like, dark blue-green leaves **Height:** 18–24" **Spread:** 4–8"

Leeks can rival most ornamental grasses for garden presence. The plants are strongly upright with stunning, dark blue-green leaves that arch from the main stem. Planted in a small group, they are a welcome addition to the border.

Don't feel you have to harvest all your leeks in fall. Some plants can be left in place to be harvested in spring or even left to flower and go to seed. These perennial plants will return year after year, and new seedlings can be allowed to grow in to replace fading plants.

Starting

Leeks can be sown directly in the garden, but because they take a long time to mature, they can also be started indoors 8 to 10 weeks before you plant them outdoors. To get off to a quicker start, purchase plants at a garden center or nursery. In areas with cool winters, set them out in spring; in warm winter regions, plant in fall.

Growing

Leeks favor **full sun** but need some shade in hot areas. The soil should be **fertile** and **well drained**, but plants adapt to most well-drained soils. Improve soil by mixing in compost or adding a layer of compost mulch once you have planted. Mounding mulch, soil or straw up around the base of the plant as summer progresses encourages tender, white growth low on the plant.

Harvesting

Leeks can be harvested as they mature, four to seven months after planting, when stems reach 1–2" in diameter. Harvest them as needed until the ground begins to freeze. In areas where winters are warm, simply leave them in the ground. Dig them up gently with a garden fork. They keep for several weeks in the refrigerator if you cut the roots short and wrap the leeks in plastic. Freeze them for longer storage, but double bag them so their onion-like flavor doesn't seep into any other food you have in the freezer.

Tips

Leeks are one of the most ornamental onions. They have bright blue-green leaves that cascade from the central stem. The second year after planting, they develop large, globe-shaped clusters of flowers atop 36" stems. Plant them in groups in your beds and borders.

Recommended

A. ampeloprasum subsp. *porrum* is an upright perennial with blue-green leaves that cascade from the central stem. Globe-shaped clusters of flowers are borne atop a tall stem the second year after planting. Varieties include **'Electra,' 'Large American Flag'** and **'Titan.'**

Problems and Pests

Problems with rot, mildew, smut, rust, leaf spot, onion flies and thrips can occur. Leeks experience fewer problems than onions.

Lettuce & Mesclun

Lactuca

Features: annual; ruffled leaves in shades of green, red and bronze, sometimes spotted, speckled or streaked and bicolored **Height:** 6–18" **Spread:** 6–18"

With so many types of lettuce available, you never have to eat the same salad twice. With a multitude of colors, textures and flavors, lettuce deserves a spot in every garden. A French term, mesclun has come to mean a group of greens grown and harvested together. Many creative seed mixes are available. Whether you choose a spicy or a mild blend, mesclun makes a welcome addition to salads and stir-fries, while providing a good groundcover in the garden.

Starting

In areas where winters are cool, start lettuce and mesclun directly in the garden around the last frost date. Warm-winter regions enjoy two planting seasons—one in spring and the other in fall. When planting the seeds of leaf lettuce and mesclun, make several smaller plantings spaced a week or two apart so you won't end up with more plants than you can use maturing at once.

Growing

Lettuce and mesclun grow well in **full sun, light shade** or **partial shade** in a **sheltered** location. The soil should be **fertile, moist** and **well drained**. Add plenty of compost to improve the soil, and be sure to keep your lettuce moist. Lettuce is very prone to drying out in hot and windy situations, so it is best to plant it where it will get some protection from other plants. Plants under too much stress can quickly bolt and go to seed or simply wilt and die.

Harvesting

Head-forming lettuce can be harvested once the head is plump. If the weather turns very hot, you may wish to cut heads even earlier because the leaves develop a bitter flavor once plants go to flower. Loose-leaf lettuce and mesclun can be harvested by pulling a few leaves off as needed or by cutting an entire plant 2–4" above ground level. Most will continue to produce new leaves even if cut this way.

Tips

Lettuce and mesclun make interesting additions to container plantings, either alone or combined with other plants. In beds and borders, mesclun makes a decorative edging plant. All lettuces and mesclun are fairly low growing and should be planted near the front of a border for casual picking.

Recommended

L. sativa forms a clump of ruffle-edged leaves and comes in many forms. Loose-leaf lettuce forms a loose rosette of leaves rather than a central head and is more heat-tolerant than others. Butter-head or Boston lettuce forms a loose head and has a very mild flavor. Compact **'Oakleaf'** has oak-shaped leaves; **'Mighty Red Oak'** is tinged with red. Slow to bolt, **'Buttercrunch'** has thick, light green outer leaves and a creamy white interior. An All American Selection, it's suitable for spring and fall crops. Crisphead or iceberg lettuce forms a very tight head of leaves. This variety does well where temperatures are moderate but may be difficult in hot-summer regions. Romaine or cos lettuce has a more upright habit, and the heads are fairly loose but cylindrical in shape. Virus-resistant **'Parris Island'** grows to 11". Dark green **'Valmaine'** produces heads 10" heads.

Mesclun mixes can be a combination of different lettuces, usually loose-leaf types, eaten while very young and tender. Mixes often also include other species of plants, including mustards, broccoli, radicchio, endive, arugula, chicory and spinach. Seed catalogs offer a good selection of pre-mixed mesclun as well as separate selections to create your own mix. **'Mild Mesclun'** has red and green leaf lettuces plus Asian greens; **'Misticanza'** includes 14 Italian lettuces.

Problems and Pests

Problems with root rot, leaf spot, flea beetles and mosaic virus can occur.

Marigolds

Tagetes

Features: annual; fragrant foliage; yellow, red, orange, brown, gold, cream or bicolored, edible flowers **Height:** 6–36" **Spread:** 6–24"

From the large, exotic, ruffled flowers of African marigold to the tiny flowers of the low-growing signet marigold, the fresh scent and warm colors of these plants add a festive touch to the garden.

Starting

Marigolds can be sown directly in the garden around the last frost date. Plants can also be purchased from garden centers and nurseries.

Growing

Marigolds grow best in **full sun**. The soil should be of **average fertility** and **well drained**. These plants are drought tolerant but hold up well in windy, rainy weather. Deadhead to prolong blooming and to keep plants tidy.

Harvesting

Flowers should be picked for use once they are fully open. Leaves of signet, lemon mint and Mexican mint marigolds can be used for teas, soups and salads.

Tips

Dot these plants in small groups throughout your beds and borders for a pretty display and to take advantage of their reputed nematode-repelling properties. Marigolds also make lovely additions to sunny container plantings.

Recommended

T. erecta (Aztec marigold, African marigold), *T. patula* (French marigold) and their hybrids have edible flowers. *T. lemmonii* (lemon mint marigold),

T. lucida (Mexican mint marigold, Mexican mint tarragon) and *T. tenuifolia* (signet marigold) are the most common culinary species.

Problems and Pests

Slugs and snails can ravage the foliage of all marigolds.

Melons

Cucumis

Features: frost-tender, trailing or climbing, annual vine; attractive foliage; yellow flowers **Height:** 12" **Spread:** 5–10'

A sweet melon off the vine—wow! Most types need consistent heat over several months. Look for varieties suitable for your region and be ready to give the heavy fruit some support.

Starting

Melons can be started indoors about six weeks before you want to transplant them to the garden. They don't like to have their roots disturbed, so plant them in fairly large peat pots so they have plenty of room to grow and can be set directly in the garden once the weather warms up. To direct sow, wait until two weeks after the last frost.

Growing

Melons grow best in **full sun** in a warm location. Plant them near a sunny wall to capture reflected heat. The soil should be **average to fertile**, **humus rich**, **moist** and **well drained**. Fruit develops poorly with inconsistent moisture, and plants can rot in cool or soggy soil. The fruit will be sweeter and more flavorful if you cut back on watering as it is ripening.

Melons have a well-deserved reputation for spreading, but like most vine-forming plants, they can be trained to grow up rather than out. Support the fruit as it becomes larger so the vines don't get damaged. Create hammocks out of old pantyhose for support.

Harvesting

Melons should be allowed to fully mature on the vine. Muskmelons develop more netting on the rind as they ripen. They generally slip easily from the vine with gentle pressure when ripe. Honeydew melons develop a paler color when they are ripe. They must be cut from the vine when they are ready.

Tips

Melons have attractive foliage and can be left to wind through your ornamental beds and borders. Trellis-supported plants, however, have fewer problems with mildew and pests.

Recommended

C. melo subsp. *indorus* (honeydew melon) and *C. melo* subsp. *reticulatus*

(muskmelon) are tender annual vines with attractive green leaves. Bright yellow flowers are produced in summer. Male and female flowers are produced separately on the same vine. The melons are round and green or gold, and some, usually muskmelons, develop a corky tan or greenish netting as they ripen. Honeydew melons develop pale green or yellow-colored flesh and require greater periods of prolonged heat than muskmelons. Two honeydew cultivars are **'Honeypearl'** and **'Saturno.'** Muskmelons generally develop orange- or salmon-colored flesh. **'Ambrosia,' 'Earliqueen,' 'Samson'** and **'Saticoy Hybrid'** are muskmelon varieties. Most melons take 70 to 85 days to produce mature, ripe fruit.

Problems and Pests

Powdery mildew, *fusarium* wilt, cucumber beetles and sap beetles can be serious problems. Mildew weakens the plants, and the beetles may introduce wilt, which is fatal.

Mint

Mentha

Features: perennial herb; upright habit; white, purple or blue flowers; green or green-and-white variegated leaves **Height:** 1"–3' **Spread:** 5–10'

Prized for its spicy-sweet leaves, mint can be invasive. Corral its enthusiasm in a container. The fragrant leaves may smell like apple, pineapple or chocolate.

Starting
Mint can be difficult to grow from seed, so buy container-grown plants or plant runners from fellow gardeners.

Growing
Depending on the variety, mint grows in **sun** or **partial shade**. Mint prefers fertile, well-drained soil. Keep the soil **moist** until plants are established. Mint grows by rapidly spreading runners, which can overtake your garden. Plant it separately in containers, or nestle bottomless containers directly in the ground to keep mint tamed. Trim the flowers, which appear from June through September, to keep the plant compact. Mint will withstand some frost but generally dies back where winters are cold. In areas with warm winters, mint will survive but may be dormant.

Harvesting
Pinch leaves when needed, which also promotes bushiness.

Tips
Mint is delightful but invasive. Try growing it in a container of mixed herbs to keep it within bounds.

Recommended
M. gentiles (apple mint) has green and white variegated leaves. It grows 1–3' tall and may spread to 3'. Apple mint tolerates more humidity than other varieties.

M. piperita (peppermint) has a reddish purple stem, small purple flowers and dark green leaves. It grows to 3' tall.

M. spicata (spearmint) has smaller, sweeter leaves than peppermint. It is the first choice for many culinary uses. The tubular flowers may be pink, white or purple.

Problems and Pests
Protect mint from whiteflies, snails, slugs and spider mites. Few diseases bother this plant.

Nasturtiums

Tropaeolum

Features: bushy or trailing annual; attractive, edible foliage; red, orange, yellow, burgundy, pink, cream, gold, white or bicolored, edible flowers **Height:** 12–18" for dwarf varieties; up to 10' for trailing varieties **Spread:** equal to height

These fast-growing, brightly colored flowers are easy to grow, making them popular with beginners and experienced gardeners alike. Native to South America, nasturtiums have a peppery flavor.

Starting

Direct sow seed once the danger of frost has passed. Where winters are warm, sow in fall for blooms in winter and spring.

Growing

Nasturtiums prefer **full sun** but tolerate some shade. The soil should be of **poor to average fertility**, **light**, **moist** and **well drained**. Rich, over-fertilized soil results in lots of leaves and very few flowers. Let the soil drain completely between waterings.

Harvesting

Pick leaves and flowers for fresh use as needed.

Tips

Nasturtiums are used in beds, borders, containers and hanging baskets and on sloped banks. Grow the climbing varieties up trellises, over rock walls or around places that you want to conceal. These problem-solvers thrive in poor locations where other plants refuse to grow and can quickly camouflage hard-to-mow slopes.

Recommended

T. majus has a trailing habit, but many cultivars have bushier, more refined habits. Cultivars offer differing flower colors or variegated foliage.

Problems and Pests

These plants rarely suffer from any problems.

Okra

Abelmoschus

Features: bushy annual; attractive foliage, flowers and fruit **Height:** 2–6'
Spread: 2'

Native to Asia, okra is a heavy producer often fried or used in soups
and stews. Grown in summer, okra sports beautiful flowers similar to
those of its cousin, hibiscus.

Starting

Okra germinates quickly in warm soil. Soak seeds overnight before planting to improve germination. Start them in peat pots six to eight weeks before you plan to move them to the garden. Wait until the last frost date has passed and the soil has warmed before moving them outside. In warmer areas, direct sow in spring.

Growing

Okra grows best in **full sun** in a **warm, sheltered** location. The soil should be **fertile, moist** and **well drained**.

Harvesting

This plant can be spiny, so wear gloves when harvesting. Okra is picked when still immature, usually a week or two after the flower drops and the pod sets. Harvest pods when they are about 3–4" long. Okra grows fast; keep the pods picked or they will turn tough.

Tips

This plant makes an attractive addition to container plantings, with the added bonus that you can extend your growing season by bringing the entire container indoors when cool weather or frost is expected.

Recommended

A. esculentus is a bushy, upright plant with sometimes spiny foliage and brown- or purple-spotted, yellow, hibiscus-like flowers. Flowers are borne at the base of each leaf where it attaches to the stem. Plants mature about 50 days after being transplanted. **'Burgundy'** is a striking heirloom with outstanding ornamental value and burgundy pods. **'Cajun Delight'** features horizontal branches that make pods easier to pick. **'Clemson Spineless'** is an All American Selections winner.

Problems and Pests

Occasional problems with slugs, spider mites, whiteflies, cabbage white

butterfly larvae, fungal leaf spot or powdery mildew can occur.

Onions

Allium

Features: biennial or perennial; upright, tubular, green leaves; globe-like flower clusters **Height:** 18–24" **Spread:** 2–4"

Onions are among the oldest cultivated plants and have been grown for so long—more than 5000 years—that their country of origin has been forgotten. They are well worth growing; many of the more interesting varieties aren't available in the supermarket. Day length and heat requirements vary. Ask your favorite nursery what types do well in your area.

Starting

Onions can be started from seed indoors about six to eight weeks before you plan to plant them outdoors; they can also be sown directly in the garden once the last frost date has passed. For a faster start, plant onion sets—small bulbs that are less than 1" wide. Bunching onions, also known as scallions, are usually started from seed sown directly in the garden. They are quick to mature, so make several smaller sowings two or three weeks apart from spring to mid-summer for a regular supply.

Growing

Onions need **full sun.** The soil should be **fertile, moist** and **well drained**. Onions use plenty of water but rot in very wet soil. They are poor at competing with other plants, so keep them well weeded. A good layer of mulch will conserve moisture and keep the weeds down. Be sure to water during periods of extended drought.

Harvesting

All onions can be harvested and used as needed throughout the season. Pull up onions that need thinning, and just pinch back the tops if you want the bulbs to mature or the plant to continue to produce leaves.

Bulb onions grown for storage are ready to be harvested when the leaves begin to yellow and flop over and the shoulders of the bulbs are just visible above the soil line. They should be pulled up and allowed to dry for a few days before being stored in a dry, cold, frost-free spot.

Onions are perennials and can also be left in the ground over winter, though the flavor can become quite strong the second year. They will flower the second summer.

Tips

Onions have fascinating cylindrical leaves that add an interesting vertical accent to the garden. Include them in beds and borders. If you want big bulbs, don't let other plants crowd them; if you want smaller bulbs, pack them in.

Recommended

A. cepa (bulb onion) forms a clump of cylindrical foliage and develops a large, round or flattened bulb. Bulb formation is day-length dependent.

The Vegetable Research and Information Center at the University of California at Davis recommends that those who live north of Bakersfield plant early types in November through January for spring or summer harvest and plant late types from January through March for harvest in summer or fall. If you're gardening south of Bakersfield, plant early varieties in October and harvest in June. Late varieties are not recommended in the south. Long-day (late) cultivars include **'Fiesta,' 'Southport,' 'Stockton Yellow'** and **'Sweet Spanish.'** Short-day (early) recommendations include **'California Early Red,' 'Granex'** and **'Grano.'**

A. fistulosum (bunching onion, green onion, shallot) is a perennial that forms a clump of foliage. The plant quickly begins to divide and multiply from the base. Plants may develop small bulbs or no bulbs at all. Once established, these plants will provide green onions all spring and summer. Try **'Evergreen White,' 'Southport White'** and **'White Lisbon.'**

Problems and Pests

Problems with smut, onion maggots and rot can occur.

Onions also make useful additions to container plantings, particularly those located conveniently near the house.

Oregano & Marjoram

Origanum

Features: fragrant foliage; white or pink, summer flowers **Height:** 12–32"
Spread: 8–18"

Relatives of mint, oregano and marjoram are two of the best-known and most frequently used herbs. They are popular in stuffings, soups and stews, and no pizza is complete until sprinkled with fresh or dried oregano.

Starting

Start oregano and marjoram from seed four to six weeks before planting them in the garden, or buy seedlings.

Growing

Oregano and marjoram grow best in **full sun**. The soil should be **average to fertile**, **neutral to alkaline** and **well drained**. They are somewhat drought tolerant once established, and keeping them on the dry side concentrates flavor. The flowers attract pollinators and beneficial insects to the garden. New wood is most productive, so cut plants back in winter or spring. Oregano may self-seed.

Harvesting

Pick leaves as needed and use them immediately or dry them for later use.

Tips

These bushy perennials make lovely additions to any border and can be trimmed to form low hedges.

Recommended

O. majorana (marjoram) is upright and shrubby. It has fuzzy, light green leaves and bears white or pink flowers in summer. Where it is not hardy, it can be grown as an annual.

O. vulgare var. *hirtum* (oregano, Greek oregano) is the most flavorful culinary variety of oregano. This low, bushy plant has fuzzy, gray-green leaves and bears white flowers. Many other interesting varieties of *O. vulgare* are available, including those with golden, variegated or curly leaves.

Problems and Pests

Problems with oregano and marjoram are rare.

Oriental Cabbage
Bok Choi
Brassica

Features: upright, leafy annual **Height:** 18" **Spread:** 12"

A tasty ingredient in stir-fries and soups, Oriental cabbage is an interesting addition to the garden. It has light or dark green, white-veined leaves with undulating or ruffled edges.

Starting

Start seeds indoors four to six weeks before the last frost date. Transplant young plants outdoors once the last frost date has passed and the soil has warmed up. Where winters are mild, plant again in the summer or fall for a later harvest.

Growing

Oriental cabbage grows best in **full sun**. The soil should be **fertile, moist** and **well drained**. Mulch to keep the soil moist.

Harvesting

A fast grower, Oriental cabbage is ready for harvest in 40 to 50 days. It comes in two basic forms: solid heads that are removed whole, and loose heads with leaves that are removed as needed.

Tips

Grow Oriental cabbage in containers, and combine it with other edible or flowering plants. Dotted through a border, it creates a low but upright feature, adding unique color and form. A slim, reliable performer, this cabbage adds ornamental and culinary value without eating up a lot of space.

Recommended

B. rapa* subsp. *chinensis (pac choi, bok choi) forms a loose clump of blue-green leaves with thick, fleshy, white or light green stems.

B. rapa* subsp. *pekinensis (Chinese cabbage) forms a dense head of tightly packed leaves.

Problems and Pests

Cutworms, leaf miners, caterpillars, root maggots, cabbage white butterfly larvae, white rust, downy mildew and powdery mildew can be problems.

Many seed catalogs offer a selection of Oriental vegetables. Some of them are cultivars or species of plants we recognize; others are unique. Try a few to expand your vegetable repertoire.

Parsley

Petroselinum

Features: biennial grown as an annual; bushy habit; attractive foliage **Height:** 8–24" **Spread:** 12–24"

Parsley is far more than an attractive garnish. Tasty and packed with vitamins, it brightens the flavor of many dishes. Try it as a tall, lovely and useful addition to a container planting.

Starting

Sow parsley directly in the garden once the last frost date has passed. Soaking the seeds for 24 hours improves germination. Transplants are also readily available.

Growing

Parsley grows well in **full sun** or **partial shade**. The soil should be **average to fertile**, **humus rich**, **moist** and **well drained**.

Harvesting

Pinch parsley to encourage bushy growth. If you cut it back regularly, it will sprout new growth.

Tips

Keep containers of parsley close to the house for easy picking. The bright green leaves and compact habit make parsley a good edging plant for beds and borders.

Recommended

P. crispum forms a clump of bright green, divided leaves. This biennial is usually grown as an annual. Cultivars may have flat or curly leaves. Flat leaves are tastier, and curly ones are more decorative. Dwarf cultivars are also available.

Problems and Pests

Parsley rarely suffers from any problems.

A nutritious addition to a variety of dishes, parsley contains vitamins A and C as well as iron.

Parsnips

Pastinaca

Features: biennial grown as an annual; sweet, edible root; feathery foliage
Height: 12–18" **Spread:** 6–8"

A root vegetable related to the carrot, parsnip imparts a smooth, sweet earthy flavor to soups and stews. Rich in potassium, it is also delicious peeled and roasted with a little garlic and olive oil. Parsnip has not reached its full potential in the states, though Europeans have enjoyed this vegetable since the days of the Roman Empire.

Starting

Where winters are cold, sow seeds in spring. In warm-winter regions, plant in fall. Cold makes parsnips sweeter. Roots may grow as deep as 15", so make sure your soil is well cultivated. Soak seeds for 24 hours before planting to improve germination.

Growing

Parsnips grow best in **full sun** but tolerate some light shade. The soil should be of **average fertility, moist** and **well drained**. Be sure to work the soil well and mix in compost to improve the texture. Roots develop poorly in heavy soil. Mulch to suppress weed growth and to conserve moisture.

Harvesting

The roots can be pulled up in fall or spring, depending on planting time. Frost improves the flavor because some of the root starches are converted to sugar in freezing weather.

Tips

Not the most ornamental of vegetables, parsnips provide a nice dark, leafy background to lower-growing plants and produce plenty of vegetables for very little effort. They impart delicious flavor to soups and stews and become even better when roasted.

Recommended

P. sativa is an upright plant with dark green, divided leaves. It develops a long, pale creamy yellow root that looks like a carrot. **'All American,' 'Gladiator,' 'Harris Model'** and **'Hollow Crown'** are commonly available cultivars.

Problems and Pests

Canker, carrot rust fly and onion maggot can affect parsnips.

Parsnips have more vitamin C than carrots.

P. sativa

Roasting the roots brings out their sweetness. Combine parsnips with potatoes, carrots and other root vegetables, then drizzle with oil and sprinkle with herbs before roasting for an hour, or until the vegetables are tender.

Peaches & Nectarines

Prunus

Features: deciduous tree; stone fruit ranges in color from red to pale gold
Height: 5–25' **Spread:** 5–25'

With careful attention to the chill factor, peaches and nectarines can be grown throughout California. Choose varieties for your region from local or mail-order nurseries. Dwarf and semi-dwarf trees are recommended for home gardens.

Peaches and nectarines have several similarities. They require the same care and are available in freestone and clingstone varieties. What's the difference? Peaches are fuzzy and nectarines are smooth. Peaches and nectarines bear in their second year, much quicker than other types of fruit trees.

P. persica 'O'Henry'

Starting

Choose a straight bare-root or container tree. Do not plant it any deeper than the soil line on the tree. Good drainage is essential. Be sure to mulch.

Growing

Peaches and nectarines need **full sun** and prefer **sandy, well-drained** soil. They must be kept consistently **moist,** especially during the growing season. Dwarf and semi-dwarf trees work well in containers. Peaches and nectarines are self-fruiting and do not require another tree for pollination.

Harvesting

Peaches and nectarines ripen from June to September, depending whether they are early, mid-season or late varieties. Look for peaches and nectarines on two-year-old trees.

Tips

Keep trees well trimmed because peaches bear on new wood and to make the fruit easier to pick. Mulch around the base of the tree. For the best result, make sure your selection suits your geographic region.

Recommended

P. persica is a tree of varying height with ripe fruit from June through September; some varieties also have lovely, fragrant flowers. Standard trees reach 15–25' tall and wide, semi-dwarf trees grow 8–12' tall and 10–12' wide, and dwarf trees grow 5–6' and 5–9' wide. Choose from an extensive selection based on region, chill hours and harvest time.

For cool areas, the following high-chill (500 hours and above) varieties are suitable. Nectarines include the sweet, white-fleshed **'Artic Glo'**; freestone, red-yellow skinned **'Fantasia'**; and juicy, large **'Goldmine,'** a taste-test winner. Peach lovers should consider the heavy-bearing heirloom **'Babcock'**; heavy-producing, delicious **'Fairtime'**; dependable, dark red **'O'Henry'**; and late-season, large, sweet **'Snow Beauty.'**

Where temperatures remain higher, look for low-chill (less than 500 hours) types. For nectarines, consider the early-ripening **'Arctic Star,'** with sweet white flesh; heavy-producing, red-skinned **'Desert Dawn'**; freestone, intensely flavored **'Pantamint'**; and early-season, freestone, sweet **'Silver Lode.'** Peach lovers might like the versatile freestone **'August Pride'**; **'Donut,'** with an unusual flattened shape and white flesh; freestone July-ripening **'Double Delight™,'** with delicious yellow fruit and beautiful pink flowers; **'Red Baron,'** with gorgeous red and pink flowers; and sweet, early-ripening cling **'Desert Gold.'**

Problems and Pests

Diseases include the fungi brown rot and peach leaf curl.

Pears

Pyrus

Features: deciduous tree; yellow, red or green fruit; attractive glossy green leaves; white flowers **Height:** 5–40' **Spread:** 5–40'

Pears grow throughout California but require winter chill for the best quality. Choose low-chill varieties where winters are warm. Delicious eaten raw or baked, pears are decorative, fruitful additions to the garden. Dwarf and semi-dwarf trees are recommended for home gardens.

Starting

Choose a straight bare-root or container tree and spread the roots over a compost layer. Do not plant any deeper than the soil line on the tree.

Growing

Pears need **full sun** and **slightly acidic, well-drained** soil. Most need cross-pollination, so plant at least two varieties. Pears need to be kept consistently **moist,** especially during the growing season. Dwarf and semi-dwarf trees work well in containers.

Harvesting

Pears ripen from July to October, depending whether they are early, mid-season or late varieties. Take fruit off the tree before it is fully ripe to avoid damage.

Tips

Trim trees for easier picking. When space is limited, espalier the tree along a sunny wall or fence. You'll get pears without the bulk of the tree.

Recommended

Standard trees grow 25–40' tall and 30–40' wide; semi-dwarf trees reach 12–16' tall and wide, and dwarf trees grow 5–8' tall and 5–9' wide.

P. communis (European) pear has a pyramid-like shape, bright green leaves and yellow, green or red fruit.

P. pyrifolia and *P. ussuriensis* (Asian) pears are rounder and crisper than European varieties. Because they require fewer chill hours, they are frequently bred with European pears to produce trees that do well in warmer climates.

Most pear varieties require lengthy chill hours for the best production and do well in the mid- to northern part of the state. Choose from European cultivars such as the well-known, delicious yellow '**Bartlett**' or its red-skinned relative, '**Sensation**'; heavy-bearing, mid-season '**Bosc**'; winter-bearing '**D'Anjou**'; and sweet, flavorful '**Seckel**.' In southern California, try juicy '**Flordahome**.'

Asian hybrids grow well in southern California. Try crisp, mid-season '**Fan Stil**' and heavy-producing '**Orient**.'

Problems and Pests

Of all fruit trees, pears have the most problems with pests and require fungicide or dormant oil spray to keep them healthy. Fireblight and codling moths can also bother pears.

Peas

Pisum

Features: climbing annual; bright green foliage; white flowers **Height:** 1–5'
Spread: 4–8"

It's easy to love peas. They are simple to grow (as long as the weather is cool), versatile, tasty and easy to store. Whether you long for the fresh flavor of shelling peas or the satisfying crunch of snap peas, they will grow well in California provided you plant to take advantage of cooler temperatures. In some areas, you may get two crops.

Starting

Peas show an admirable appreciation for cool weather. Where winters are cold, you may get two crops by planting in early spring and in fall about 12 weeks before the first frost. In regions with warm winters, plant in fall. Peas mature in 60 to 70 days; count backwards to make sure they don't ripen in the heat of summer. Peas, like beans, can be treated with bacterial inoculants before planting to ensure a good supply of nitrogen-fixing bacteria on the roots.

Growing

Peas grow well in **full sun**. The soil should be **average to fertile, humus rich, moist** and **well drained**. Both bush and vining peas are available. Bush types do not need support. For vining peas, provide support such as twiggy branches, nets or chain-link fences for the small, twining tendrils. Base your support height on the expected plant height, and make sure it is in place before your seeds sprout because the roots are quite shallow and damage easily.

Harvesting

Harvest peas when they're still young and tender. To avoid damaging the plant, use two hands to harvest—one to hold the vine and the other to pull the pea pod. The more you pick, the more peas the plants produce.

Tips

Peas make excellent privacy plants. They will grow easily up a low chain-link fence, and the taller varieties create a privacy screen quite quickly. Low-growing and medium-height peas make interesting additions to hanging baskets and container plantings. They grow up the hangers or supports or spill over the edges and trail down.

Recommended

P. sativum var. *sativum* are climbing plants with bright green, waxy stems and leaves and white flowers. The resulting pods are grouped into three categories: shelling peas, snow peas and snap peas. The seeds are removed from the pods of shelling peas and are the only part eaten. Snow peas are eaten as flat, seedless pods. Snap peas develop fat seeds, and the pod and seeds are eaten together. Vining types work best along the coast.

Shelling pea choices include small bush types **'Laxton's Progress,'** a vigorous dwarf vine with 4–5" pods, and **'Little Marvel,'** with peas that hold well on the vine.

Vining selections include **'Green Marvel,'** a disease-resistant variety with double pods and 2' vines; and productive, disease-resistant **'Maestro,'** also with 2' vines.

Snow pea varieties include **'Dwarf Grey Sugar,'** a bush type with purple blossoms that reaches 3' high, and **'Mammoth Melting Sugar,'** whose pods are 4–5" long and ¾" wide.

If you're interested in snap peas, consider the disease-resistant **'Sugar Ann'**; **'Sugar Daddy,'** a cross between a green pea and a snow pea that results in a stringless snap pea; and **'Super Sugar Snap,'** with plump pods and high yields.

Problems and Pests

Peas are prone to powdery mildew, so choose disease-resistant varieties, and avoid touching the plants when they are wet to prevent the spread of disease. Aphids and whiteflies can also cause problems.

Peppers
Capsicum

Features: bushy annual; attractive foliage; white flowers; colorful fruit **Height:** 1–4'
Spread: 12–18"

The variety of sweet and chili peppers is nothing short of remarkable. With all the different shapes, colors and flavors, you're sure to find some favorites.

Starting

Peppers need warmth to germinate and grow. Start seeds indoors 6 to 10 weeks before the last frost date. Plant seedlings or purchased container plants outside in a warm, sunny location when temperatures remain above 50° F.

Growing

Peppers grow best in **full sun** in a warm location. The soil should be **average to fertile, moist** and **well drained**. Mulch to keep them moist because peppers need heat to thrive and can dry out quickly.

Harvesting

For the fullest flavor, pick peppers when they are ripe. They will continue ripening after they have been picked. Chili peppers can also be dried.

Tips

Pepper plants are neat and bushy. Once peppers set and begin to ripen, the plants get colorful as the bright red, orange and yellow fruit contrasts beautifully with the dark green foliage. All peppers are good additions to container plantings. Chili peppers in particular are useful in containers because they

usually have the most interesting shapes. Some smaller chili peppers make good houseplants for warm, sunny windows.

Recommended

C. annuum is the most common species of sweet and hot peppers. Plants are bushy with dark green foliage. Flowers are white, and peppers can be shades of green, red, orange, yellow, purple or brown. Cultivars of sweet peppers include **'California Wonder,' 'King of the North,' 'Purple Beauty,' 'Red Mini Bell'** and **'Yankee Bell.'** Cultivars of chili peppers include **'Anaheim,' 'Cayenne,' 'Jalapeno,' 'Scotch Bonnet'** and **'Thai,'** just to name a few.

C. chinense 'Habanero' is one of the hottest chili peppers. It is native to the Caribbean.

Problems and Pests
Rare problems with aphids and white-flies can occur.

Capsaicin is the chemical that gives peppers their heat. Pepper heat is measured in Scoville units; the higher the unit number, the hotter the peppers. Sweet peppers have about 100 Scoville units; habaneros can have up to 350,000.

Persimmons

Diospyros

Features: deciduous tree; yellow-orange or red-orange fruit; green leaves turn yellow, orange or red in fall **Height:** 20–30' **Spread:** 8–10'

Persimmons thrive throughout California and do not require much winter chilling. Of the two varieties—American and Oriental—the latter is more commonly grown in the state and has the largest fruit.

Starting

Choose a straight bare-root or container tree and plant it, spreading the roots over a compost layer. Do not plant any deeper than the soil line on the tree. Persimmons have a tap root, so dig a deep hole to accommodate it.

Growing

Persimmons need **full sun**. They tolerate a variety of soil conditions but prefer **loamy, well-drained** soil. Keep persimmons consistently **moist,** especially during the growing season. Some varieties need cross-pollination. They may take up to seven years to bear fruit.

Standard trees grow 20–30' tall but can be trimmed to 8' or less to make the fruit easier to pick and for better placement in home gardens.

Harvesting

Persimmons ripen from October through November.

Tips

Keep birds, bats and possums from destroying your fruit by draping a soft net over your tree.

Recommended

D. kaki is the Oriental type and can grow to 30', though trimming and smaller cultivars make it suitable for home gardens. Green oval leaves turn orange and red in fall. Some fruit is soft and sweet; other varieties are firm and more like apples in texture. Try the popular, firm **'Fuyu'** and the large, soft **'Hachiya.'**

Problems and Pests

Persimmons have few problems with pests.

With leaves that change color and gorgeous orange-red fruit, persimmons are prized for their ornamental value as well as their delicious fruit.

D. kaki 'Fuyu' (both photos)

Plums

Prunus

Features: deciduous tree; stone fruit ranging in color from green to red to purple
Height: 5–25' **Spread:** 5–25'

There are two types of plums: Japanese and European. We're most familiar with the former, which blooms and matures earlier and has larger, firmer fruit and greater disease resistance. Both types yield fruit in 140 to 170 days. With careful attention to the chill factor, plums can be grown throughout California.

P. domestica 'Elephant Heart'

Starting

Choose a straight bare-root or container-grown tree. Do not plant it any deeper than the soil line on the tree.

Growing

Plums need **full sun.** They prefer **well-drained, humus-rich** soil. Most are self-fruiting, while others require pollinators to produce fruit. Good drainage is essential. Be sure to mulch.

Harvesting

Plums ripen from June to September, depending whether they are early, mid-season or late varieties.

Tips

Plums are easy to grow. They tolerate wet soil and fruit late enough to avoid frost problems. For the best results, make sure your selection suits your geographic region. Dwarf and semi-dwarf trees are recommended for gardens. Trim trees for easier picking.

Recommended

Standard trees grow 20–25' tall and wide, semi-dwarf trees reach 8–14' tall and 8–12' wide, and dwarf trees have a height and spread of 5–10'.

P. domestica (European plum) is larger and requires more chill hours than Japanese plum. For cooler areas with 500 chill hours and above, consider purple-skinned **'Autumn Beauty'**; purple, juicy, heavy-bearing **'Elephant Heart'**; delicious, yellow-fleshed **'Golden Nectar'**; and California favorite **'Santa Rosa.'**

Where temperatures remain higher, look for low-chill (less than 500 hours) types such as the coastal producer **'Beauty'**; long-season **'Burgundy,'** which bears fruit from July to August; juicy, freestone, yellow **'Howard Miracle'**; **'Santa Rosa'**; and sweet, meaty **'Satsuma.'**

P. salicina (Japanese plum) is a tree of varying height with ripe fruit from June through September; some varieties also have lovely, fragrant flowers. Skin and flesh color range from dark purple to red to green. Early, mid-season and late varieties are available. Choose from an extensive selection based on region, chill hours and harvest time.

Problems and Pests

Plums have fewer problems than apples or peaches, though they may experience diseases including brown rot and scale.

Poppies

Papaver

Features: red, pink, white or purple, single or double flowers; edible seeds
Height: 1–4' **Spread:** 8–18"

Poppy seeds are frequently added to baked goods. Remarkably easy to grow, poppies also add abundant color to your garden.

Starting

Direct sow poppies in spring. Where
winters are mild, plant in fall. Several
successive, smaller sowings will give
you a longer flower display, but it's not
necessary if you are growing poppies for
the seeds. The seeds are very small; mix
them with fine sand before you plant.
Because they need light to germinate,
don't cover the seeds.

Growing

Poppies grow best in **full sun**. The soil
should be **fertile, sandy, humus rich** and
well drained.

Harvesting

Seeds are ready to harvest when the
pods begin to dry. Shake the pods and if
the seeds rattle, they're ready. Cut the
pod heads off and shake the seeds into
a paper bag. Dry them and store them
in a container.

Tips

Poppies work well in mixed borders.
They fill empty spaces early in the season then die back, leaving room for
other plants. They also self-seed freely
and are likely to continue to spring up
in your garden.

Recommended

P. somniferum (opium poppy) forms
a basal rosette of foliage. Leafy stems
bear red, pink, white or purple flowers.
Large, blue-green seedpods follow the

P. somniferum (photos this page)

flowers. Propagation of the species is
restricted in many countries because of
its narcotic properties, but several acceptable cultivars are available for ornamental and culinary purposes. Blue-,
white- or brown-seeded varieties are
available.

Problems and Pests

Poppies rarely suffer from any problems.

Potatoes

Solanum

Features: bushy annual; leafy, rounded habit; pink, purple or white flowers
Height: 18–24" **Spread:** 12–24"

Potatoes were cultivated in South America for centuries and were introduced to Europe by the Spanish. They arrived in North America with European immigrants.

Starting

Seed potato sets (small tubers) can be purchased and planted in spring a few weeks before the last frost date as long as the soil isn't cold and wet. Young plants can tolerate a light frost but not a hard freeze. Seed potatoes can be cut into smaller pieces as long as each has two "eyes," the dimpled spots from which the plant and roots grow. Each piece needs 12–18" of space.

Growing

Potatoes prefer **full sun** but tolerate some shade. The soil should be **fertile, humus rich, acidic, moist** and **well drained.** Mound soil up around plants to keep tubers out of the light as they develop. Potatoes have shallow root systems and should be kept moist.

Harvesting

Harvest potatoes two to four months after planting. The tubers begin to form around the same time as the plants begin to flower. After harvesting, let potatoes dry for a few hours on the soil, then brush off the dirt and store them in a cold, dark place. If you live in a no-frost area, you can keep potatoes in the ground until you need them.

Tips

These large, bushy plants with white, pink or light purple flowers are good fillers for an immature border and are excellent at breaking up the soil in newer gardens.

Recommended

S. tuberosum is a bushy, mound-forming plant. It bears tiny, exotic-looking, white, pink or light purple flowers in late summer. Many varieties of potatoes are available. They can have rough or smooth, white, yellow, brown, red or blue skin and white, yellow, purple or blue flesh. A few popular varieties include **'All-Blue,'** with smooth, blue skin and light purple-blue flesh; **'Nooksack,'** said to be a good

performer in wet areas; **'Norgold Russet,'** which is good for baking; **'White Superior,'** an early white variety; and **'Yukon Gold,'** with smooth, light beige skin and yellow flesh.

Problems and Pests

Potatoes are susceptible to a variety of diseases, including scab. Avoid planting them in the same spot two years in a row. Potato beetle is the most troublesome insect pest.

Purchase seed sets of an unusual variety rather than duplicating those from the grocery store.

All parts of the potato plant are poisonous except the tubers, and they can become poisonous if they are exposed to light. Green flesh is a good indication that your potatoes have been exposed to light. To protect your potatoes, mound soil around the plants, 1" or so per week, from midsummer to fall. A straw mulch also effectively shades developing tubers.

Quinoa

Chenopodium

Features: branching, upright annual; soft leaves; attractive flower heads; good fall color **Height:** 5–8' **Spread:** 12–18"

A protein-rich, easy-to-grow, nutty flavored grain, quinoa looks great in the garden. The colorful seed heads form in clusters at the tips of the branches. Quinoa does not set seeds well in high-heat areas.

Starting

Sow directly in the garden once the soil has dried out. Plant in spring for a fall harvest. Young plants tolerate a light frost. Seeds can be scattered over an area or planted in rows. Keep the seedbed moist during germination. Young seedlings resemble the weed lamb's quarters, so take care when weeding not to pull up the plants you want.

Growing

Quinoa grows best in **full sun** but does not like high heat. The soil should be **average to fertile** and **well drained**, though the plant adapts to most conditions and tolerates drought once established. A layer of mulch will conserve moisture and keep weeds down, but this plant's leafy habit tends to suppress weed growth once the plant starts to fill in.

Harvesting

When leaves die back, grasp the stem with a gloved hand and pull upward to remove the seeds. To remove plant bits, run your hands through the collected seeds on a lightly breezy day or blow a fan across the surface to carry away the dry plant bits. Dry the seeds completely before storing them.

Tips

This lovely, tall plant, with its seed heads that ripen to shades of gold, orange and red, is a welcome addition to the fall garden. Combine it with other tall fall bloomers, such as sunflowers and amaranth, to create a stunning display along a fence or wall.

Recommended

C. quinoa is a tall, leafy, branching annual. Flowers are borne in dense clusters along the tips of the stems. The leaves turn shades of orange and red in fall, and the seeds ripen to shades of red, orange, gold, green or pink. Seeds may be brown, yellow or white. There are many cultivars, though they can be a bit difficult to find. **'Isluga'** has yellow-gold or pink seed heads that produce plenty of yellow seeds. **'Multi-hued'** bears flowers in shades of red, orange and purple. **'Temuco'** has chartreuse and red seed heads and white seeds.

Problems and Pests

Insects and disease occasionally trouble leaves, but seed production is rarely affected.

Your plants should be 12–18" apart. If they fill in too densely, thin out extra seedlings and add to salads, or steam and serve like spinach. Young leaves can also be prepared this way.

Quinoa seeds are coated in a bitter substance called saponin. Light-colored seeds have less saponin. To wash off the substance, rinse seeds vigorously in water. The water will stop foaming when the saponin is gone. You can even put the seeds in a pillowcase or mesh bag and run them through a cycle in the washing machine (without soap) to rinse large quantities thoroughly.

Radishes
Daikon Radish
Raphanus

Features: annual; rosette of foliage; fast growing **Height:** 6–8" **Spread:** 4–6"

Radishes are grouped into two categories. Spring radishes include the familiar round and cylindrical red radishes. Winter radishes, which include Oriental, daikon and Spanish varieties, are eaten raw or cooked. The spicy pods of some Oriental radishes are also popular in salads.

Starting

Direct sow seed in spring, as soon as the soil warms up a bit and can be worked. Plants tolerate light frost. Where winters are mild, sow in fall. Successive, smaller plantings can be made every couple of weeks to ensure a steady supply.

Growing

Radishes grow well in **full sun** or **light shade**. The soil should be of **average fertility, loose, humus rich, moist** and **well drained**. Heavy or rocky soils result in a rough, woody texture and an unpleasant taste.

Harvesting

Harvest spring radishes three weeks to two months after planting, or as soon as roots develop. Flavor and texture deteriorates quickly if they are left in the ground or stored for too long.

Daikon and Spanish radishes can be stored, like carrots, in moist sand in a cool, dry location. They can also be pickled.

Tips

Easy to grow and a wonderful addition to salads, radishes are also great nurse plants. Mix them in with small-seeded or slow-to-germinate plants such as parsnips and carrots, and radishes will help them flourish by shading out weeds and reducing evaporation. Radishes sprout and mature quickly; some varieties are ready to harvest within a month.

Because of their leafy, low-growing habit, radishes make interesting edging plants for borders and are unique additions to container plantings. Use radishes for a quick-growing display that will be replaced by other plants.

Recommended

R. sativus forms a low clump of leaves. The edible roots can be long and slender or short and round; the skin can be rosy red, white or black. Try the colorful

mixed white, red and purple **'Easter Egg II,'** dependable **'French Breakfast'** and mild, white-fleshed **'Purple Plum.'**

Problems and Pests

Flea beetles and cabbage maggots are common problems for radishes.

Radishes are related to cabbage, broccoli and mustard. They were grown by the ancient Greeks and Romans.

Radishes tend to bolt in hot weather, and the roots develop an unpleasantly hot flavor. Choose icicle types for your summer growing because they are more tolerant of hot weather than the round, red varieties.

Raspberries & Blackberries

Rubus

Features: thicket-forming shrub; long, arching canes; spring flowers; summer fruit
Height: 3–10' **Spread:** 4–5' or more

These sweet, juicy berries are popular in pies, jams and other fruity desserts, but they are just as delicious eaten fresh.

Starting

Plant bare-root canes in fall, winter or early spring. Plant container-grown plants any time—just be sure to keep them moist.

Growing

Raspberries and blackberries grow well in **full sun, light shade** or **partial shade,** though the best fruiting occurs in full sun. The soil should be of **average fertility, humus rich, moist** and **well drained**. These plants prefer a location **sheltered** from strong winds.

Look for fruit the second season. Prune out some of the older canes each year once plants become established to keep plants vigorous and to control their spread. Prune and stake thickets to form neat rows, or let the canes spread freely if you have the space. Raspberries require winter chill to reach their best flavor.

The more adaptable blackberry tolerates a wider range of conditions, from high heat to cool dampness. Blackberries have very long, flexible canes. They can stand freely without staking, but they may take up less room if they are loosely tied to a supportive structure such as a stout post or fence.

Harvesting

Pick fruit as soon as it is ripe. All the fruit does not ripen at once, and you can harvest it for a month or more. Some raspberry varieties are ever-bearing and produce fruit in flushes from mid-summer through fall.

Tips

These shrubs form rather formidable thickets and can be used in shrub and mixed borders, along fences and as hedges.

Recommended

R. fruticosus (blackberries, brambles) forms a thicket of thorny stems or canes. Canes can grow up to 10' long, and thickets can spread 5' or more. White, or occasionally pink, late-spring or early-summer flowers are followed by red or black berries

in late summer. Thornless varieties are also available. Trailing types include mid-season **'Boysen,'** with soft, flavorful maroon berries that ripen in June and July; early-ripening **'Logan,'** with dark red berries that have a distinctive flavor; and well-known **'Marion,'** with large, firm, bright black berries on thorny bushes. Try erect varieties such as the thornless, mid-season **'Black Satin'**; heat-tolerant, mid-season **'Cherokee'**; early-season **'Cheyenne'**; and productive, long-season, heat-tolerant **'Shawnee.'**

R. idaeus (raspberries) forms a thicket of bristly stems or canes. Canes grow 3–5' long, and thickets can spread to 4' or more. White, spring flowers are followed by red, yellow, black or purple fruit in mid-summer. Raspberries fall into two categories: summer-bearing and ever-bearing. Although raspberry shrubs are perennial, the canes are biennial, generally growing the first

year and producing fruit the second. In the third season, the canes die back. Ever-bearing canes begin to fruit late in the season of their first fall, then again the second summer. They are suitable in regions where fall is long and warm; summer-bearing varieties are more suitable for areas with shorter seasons. Summer-bearing red raspberries include **'Haida,'** with firm, medium-red berries resistant to root rot; the nicely flavored **'Meeker'**; the productive **'Nootka,'** with firm berries; and sweet, medium-sized **'Sumner,'** the most tolerant of wet soil. Ever-bearing choices include the self-supporting, tasty **'August Red'**; early-ripening, delicious **'Autumn Bliss'**; early-ripening **'Red Wing'**; and bright-red **'September.'** Warm-area choices include **'Bababerry'** and **'Oregon 1030.'**

Problems and Pests

Problems with anthracnose, powdery mildew, rust, fire blight, *verticillium* wilt, leafhoppers and caterpillars can occur.

Spread excess fruit on a paper-lined cookie sheet and freeze it. Transfer the fruit to a plastic bag once it is frozen.

ubarb

Rh

Features: clump-forming perennial; red or green stems; large, deeply veined leaves; spikes of flowers in summer **Height:** 2–4' **Spread:** 3–6'

Like tomatoes, rhubarb treads the fine line between fruit and vegetable. We usually eat it in fruit dishes and think of it more as a fruit, but rhubarb is actually a vegetable. The leaves are poisonous.

Starting

Start plants in winter or early spring; warm-area gardeners should plant in fall. Rhubarb can be started from seed sown directly in the garden, or crowns can be purchased in spring. If you've planted crowns, you can begin harvesting the second summer. Seeded plants may take three or more years before they produce a harvest.

Rhubarb produces best with some winter chill and does particularly well along the coast and in cool Central Valley areas.

Growing

Rhubarb grows best in **full sun** or **partial shade** in warmer areas. The soil should be **fertile, humus rich, moist** and **well drained.** Gently work some compost into the soil each year, and add a layer of compost mulch. Fertile soil encourages more and bigger stems.

Rhubarb can stay in one spot for many years but will remain more vigorous and productive if divided about every eight or so years. Dig the soil over and

Although the flowers are quite interesting and attractive, they are often removed to prolong the stem harvest.

Inedible ornamental rhubarb (below)

work in some compost when you divide the plant. Break roots into small sections and plant those with at least one "eye," the small dimple from which these vegetables sprout.

Harvesting

Harvest stems by pulling firmly and cleanly from the base of the plant. Cut the leaves from the stems with a sharp knife and compost or spread them around the base of the plant to conserve moisture, suppress weed growth and return nutrients to the soil. Don't remove more than half of the stems from the plant in one year. Remove flowers quickly; plants that flower produce fewer vegetables the following year.

Tips

Sadly, this stunning plant is often relegated to back corners and waste areas in the garden. With its dramatic leaves, bright red stems and intriguing flowers, rhubarb deserves a far more central location.

Recommended

R. rhabarbarum and *R.* x *hybridum* form large clumps of glossy, deeply veined, green, bronzy or reddish leaves. The edible stems can be green, red or a bit of both. Spikes of densely clustered red, yellow or green flowers are produced in mid-summer. Popular varieties include the red-stalked **'Cherry'** and greenish-red **'Victoria.'**

Problems and Pests

Rhubarb rarely suffers from any problems.

Only the stems of rhubarb are edible. The leaves contain oxalic acid in toxic quantities.

Rosemary

Rosmarinus

Features: fragrant, evergreen foliage; bright blue, sometimes pink flowers
Height: 8"–7' **Spread:** 1–4'

The needle-like leaves of this fragrant shrub are used to flavor a wide variety of foods, including chicken, pork, lamb, rice, tomato and egg dishes. A Mediterranean native, this versatile herb performs well under a variety of conditions and has great value as a landscape plant.

Starting

Specific varieties can be purchased from garden centers, nurseries and specialty growers. Seed can be started any time.

Growing

Rosemary prefers full sun but tolerates partial shade. The soil should be of poor to average fertility and well drained. Rosemary thrives on a bit of neglect; be stingy with water and fertilizer. In cold areas, shelter it from winter winds. This plant takes well to frequent, light pruning.

Harvesting

Pick leaves as needed.

Tips

Grow rosemary as a fragrant hedge that doubles as a convenient source of fresh herbs. Rosemary attracts birds, butterflies and bees.

Recommended

R. officinalis is a dense, bushy, evergreen shrub with narrow, dark green leaves. The habit varies from strongly upright to prostrate and spreading. Flowers are usually shades of blue, but pink-flowered cultivars are available. Upright varieties include the cold-resistant, hardy **'Arp,'** which grows 4' wide and tall; **'Blue Spires,'** a 6' specimen ideal for hedges; and the famous **'Tuscan Blue,'** with violet blue flowers and a height of 6–7'. A popular prostrate variety is **'Huntington Carpet,'** which spreads 1.5' and is useful for covering banks and large areas.

Problems and Pests

Rosemary has few problems.

Rutabagas

Brassica

Features: rosette-forming biennial; edible roots; blue-green foliage **Height:** 12–24"
Spread: 4–8"

Among the tastiest root vegetables, rutabagas are not as popular as
they deserve to be. Try them in soups and stews, and enjoy their
warm, buttery, sweet flavor. A cross between cabbage and turnip,
they are also delicious when roasted with other root vegetables.
Rutabagas are a cool-season crop.

Starting

Sow seeds directly in the garden in spring. Keep the seedbed moist until the plant germinates. In warm areas, plant in fall to harvest in winter.

Growing

Rutabagas prefer to grow in **full sun**. The soil should be **fertile, moist** and **well drained**. The roots can develop discolored centers in boron-deficient soil. Work agricultural boron into the soil if needed. These plants require consistent moisture during the growing season to produce the best vegetables.

Harvesting

Harvest when the roots are 3–5" in diameter, or leave them in the ground to sweeten with cooler weather. Pull roots by hand or dig them out carefully with a garden fork.

Tips

Rutabagas grow large, bushy clumps of blue-green foliage and can be included in the middle of a border where they provide an attractive, contrasting background for other plants.

Recommended

B. napus (rutabaga, swede, winter turnip) forms a large clump of blue-green leaves. The leaves are not edible. The roots are most often white with purple tops and have yellow flesh. A few varieties are available including the popular **'American Purple Top'** and the many types of long-storing **'Laurentian.'** Choose a variation that is clubroot resistant if this disease is common in your region.

Problems and Pests

Cabbage root maggots, cabbage worms, aphids, flea beetles, rust, fungal diseases, downy mildew, powdery mildew and clubroot are possible problems.

The rutabaga originated in Europe and has been in cultivation for more than 4000 years.

Sage

Salvia

Features: shrubby perennial; fragrant, decorative foliage; red, white, pink, blue or purple flowers **Height:** 12–24" **Spread:** 18–36"

A Mediterranean herb, sage is perhaps best known as a flavoring for stuffing. The leaves are also used in soups, stews, sausages and dumplings.

Starting

Start seeds indoors in late winter or early spring, or purchase seedlings.

Growing

Sage does well in **full sun** but prefers **light shade** in the hottest areas. The soil should be of **average fertility** and **well drained**. This plant benefits from a light mulch of compost each year. Drought tolerant once established, sage forms a small, woody shrub.

Harvesting

Pick fresh leaves as needed, or dry and freeze them for later use.

Tips

Sage is a good border plant, adding volume to the middle and attractiveness to the front. It can also be grown in mixed planters.

Recommended

S. officinalis is a woody, mound-forming perennial with soft, gray-green leaves. Spikes of light purple or blue flowers appear in early and mid-summer. Many cultivars with attractive foliage are available, including the yellow-leaved **'Golden Sage,'** the yellow-margined **'Icterina,'** the purple-leaved **'Purpurea'**

and the purple, green and cream variegated **'Tricolor,'** which also has a pink flush to the new growth. **'Compacta'** is a small version perfect for containers.

Problems and Pests

Sage rarely suffers from any problems, but it can rot in wet soil.

Sorrel

Rumex

Features: low-growing perennial often grown as an annual; tangy, edible leaves
Height: 6–36" **Spread:** 12–24"

Somewhere between a salad green and an herb, sorrel features tangy, sour leaves equally at home in a bowl of mixed greens or in soups, marinades and egg dishes. Sorrel is similar to spinach but tolerates heat more successfully.

R. acetosa

Starting
Sow the seed directly in the garden in fall or spring. Set out transplants when available.

Growing
Sorrel grows well in **full sun, light shade** or **partial shade**. The soil should be **fertile, acidic, humus rich, moist** and **fairly well drained**. Mulch to conserve moisture.

Divide sorrel every three or four years to keep the plant vigorous and the leaves tender and tasty. This plant self-seeds if flowering spikes are not removed.

Harvesting
Pick leaves as needed in spring and early summer. Remove flower spikes as they emerge to prolong the leaf harvest. Once the weather warms and the plant goes to flower, the leaves lose their pleasant flavor. If you cut the plant back a bit at this point, you will have fresh leaves to harvest in late summer and fall when the weather cools again.

Tips
A tasty and decorative addition to the vegetable, herb or ornamental garden, French sorrel also makes an attractive groundcover and can be included in mixed container plantings.

Recommended
R. acetosa (garden sorrel, broad leaf sorrel) is a vigorous, clump-forming perennial. The inconspicuous flowers are borne on a tall stem that emerges from the center of the clump. This plant grows 18–36" tall and spreads about 12".

R. scutatus (French sorrel, buckler leaf sorrel) forms a low, slow-spreading clump of foliage. Stronger tasting but less plentiful than garden sorrel, the leaves hold their flavor better in warm weather. It grows 6–18" tall and spreads up to 24".

Problems and Pests
Sorrel is generally problem-free. Snails, slugs, rust and leaf spot can occasionally cause problems.

Oxalic acid gives sorrel leaves their flavor. They are safe to eat but can upset stomachs in large quantities.

Soybeans
Edamame
Glycine

Features: bushy annual; edible seeds **Height:** 12–24" **Spread:** 12–18"

Popular for years in Asian countries, protein-rich soybeans are now an American favorite for snacks, salads and more. Simmer the beans in salted water or roast them, then eat them out of the pods.

Starting

Sow seeds directly in the garden after the last frost date has passed when the soil has warmed up.

Growing

Soybeans grow best in **full sun** but tolerate some light afternoon shade. The soil should be of **average fertility** and **well drained**. Make sure they get good circulation to avoid mildew.

Harvesting

Harvest when the pods are plump and full but the seeds are still tender and green. Alternatively, grow them to maturity and dry the beans for use in soups and stews.

Tips

Soybeans are very ornamental, with attractive leaves and plentiful flowers. They can be used as low, temporary hedges or planted in small groups in a border.

Recommended

G. max is a bushy annual that produces clusters of large-seeded pods. Several soybean cultivars are available, including **'Beer Friend,' 'Black Jet,' 'Butter- baby,' 'Envy'** and **'Green Pearls.'**

Problems and Pests

Leaf spot, bacterial blight, rust, bean beetles and aphids can cause problems.

Soybeans contain all nine essential amino acids, have no cholesterol and are low in saturated fats and sodium. They are an excellent source of dietary fiber and are high in iron, calcium, B vitamins, zinc, lecithin, phosphorous and magnesium.

Spinach

Spinacia

Features: clump-forming annual; smooth or crinkled, edible leaves
Height: 12–18" **Spread:** 6–10"

Nutritious, versatile spinach stars in a variety of
dishes. A cool-season vegetable, spinach
goes to seed in warm weather.
Consider sorrel as an alternative for warm-weather
planting.

Starting

Direct sow spinach in spring as soon as the soil can be worked. In warm areas, sow in fall to take advantage of cooler temperatures.

Growing

Spinach grows well in **full sun** or **light shade** and prefers cool weather and a cool location. The soil should be **fertile, moist** and **well drained**. Add a layer of mulch to help cool the soil and delay bolting. Bolt-resistant varieties are also available.

Harvesting

Harvest spinach about seven weeks after planting. If you need just a few leaves, pick as needed. For greater quantities, cut the entire plant just above where it emerges from the ground—you may get a second crop. The flavor deteriorates as the weather heats up and the plant matures and goes to flower.

Tips

Spinach's dark green foliage is attractive when mass planted and provides a good contrast for brightly colored flowers. Try it in a nearby container for convenient harvesting.

Recommended

S. oleracea forms a dense, bushy clump of glossy, dark green, smooth or crinkled (savoyed) foliage. Plants are ready for harvest in about 45 days. Slow-bolting, savoyed **'America'** has great flavor and is ideal for spring or fall planting; an All American Selections winner, savoyed **'Melody Hybrid'** resists disease; and smooth-leaved **'Space'** is a disease-resistant variety that is ready to eat in only 50 days.

Problems and Pests

Avoid powdery and downy mildew by keeping a bit of space between each plant for good air flow.

*The unrelated New Zealand spinach (*Tetragonia expansa*) is an excellent and interesting alternative to regular spinach. Plant in summer after spinach starts to fade, and use the leaves of this heat-resistant plant in the same way. New Zealand spinach grows upright and has a branching habit.*

Squash

Cucurbita

Features: trailing or mounding annual; large lobed, decorative leaves; colorful flowers and fruit **Height:** 18–24" **Spread:** 2–10'

Native to the Americas, squash falls into two categories—summer and winter. Grown during warm weather months, summer squash includes thin-skinned varieties such as patty pan, crookneck and zucchini. They're harvested when immature and eaten immediately. Harvested in late summer or fall, thicker-skinned winter squash such as pumpkins, butternut, acorn and others are better keepers.

C. pepo flowers

Starting

Start seeds in peat pots indoors six to eight weeks before the last frost date. Transplants are also available. Plant out or direct sow after the last frost date once the soil has warmed up.

Growing

Squash grow best in **full sun** but tolerate light shade from companion plants. The soil should be **fertile, humus rich, moist** and **well drained**. Mulch to keep the soil moist and the plants dry.

Squash grows as a vine and as non-vining bushes. Where space is limited, chose bush types.

Because both male and female flowers appear on each plant, you might think pollination would be a simple matter of wind-born pollen transfer. Nature evidently had other ideas. The pollen is sticky and can only be transferred by bees (or very dedicated gardeners). Grow squash near bee-attracting herbs and flowers to increase production.

Harvesting

Summer squash are tastiest if picked and eaten when they are young. Harvest them when they are small: zucchini should be 6–8", patty pan 3–4" and crookneck 4–7" long. The more you pick, the more the plants will produce. Cut the fruit cleanly from the plant, and avoid damaging the leaves and stems to prevent disease and insect problems.

Harvest winter squash when they are mature. You should be able to press into the skin without leaving an indentation. Allow them to cure in a warm, dry place for a few weeks until the skins become thick and hard. Store them in a cool, dry place, and check regularly for spoilage.

Tips

Mound-forming squash, with their tropical-looking leaves, add interest to borders as feature plants. Train small-fruited trailing selections up trellises for vertical interest. The heavy-fruited trailing types will wind happily through a border of taller plants or shrubs. All squash can be grown in

C. pepo (above & below)

containers, but the mound-forming and shorter-trailing selections are usually the most attractive; the long-trailing types end up as a stem that leads over the edge of the container.

Recommended

Squash plants are generally similar in appearance, with medium to large leaves held on long stems. Plants are trailing in habit, but some form only very short vines, so they appear to be more mound forming. Bright yellow, trumpet-shaped male and female flowers are borne separately but on the same plant. Female flowers can be distinguished by their short stem and by the juvenile fruit at the base of the flower. Male flowers have longer stems.

Four species of squash are commonly grown in gardens. They vary incredibly in their appearance and can be smooth

or warty, round, elongated or irregular. In color, they can be dark green, tan, creamy white or bright orange, and solid, stripy or spotted. The size ranges from tiny, round zucchini that would fit in the palm of a child's hand to immense pumpkins that could hold two or three children. Experiment to find your favorite.

C. maxima includes buttercup squash and hubbard. These plants generally need 90 to 110 days to mature. They keep very well, often longer than any other squash, and have sweet, fine-textured flesh.

C. mixta includes cushaw squash and is not as well known. These plants generally take 100 days or more to mature. Some are grown for their edible seeds, while others

are used in baking and are good for muffins, loaves and pies.

C. moschata includes butternut squash and generally needs 95 or more days to mature. These squash keep well and are popular baked or for soups and stews.

C. pepo is the largest group of squash and includes summer squash, such as zucchini, and many winter squash, such as pumpkins, acorn squash, spaghetti squash, dumpling squash and gourds.

Summer squash are ready to harvest in 45 to 50 days, and the winter squash in this group take from 70 to 75 days for acorn and spaghetti squash to 95 to 120 days for some of the larger pumpkins.

Interesting summer varieties include zucchini such as **'Cocozelle,'** an heirloom bush type; **'Dark Star,'** a cross between a hybrid and an heirloom; and compact **'Ambassador'** and **'Greyzini.'** Try patty pan **'Reve Scallopini,'** with a flattened shape and dark green color;

tiny **'Peter Pan'**; and yellow **'Sunburst.'** Productive crooknecks include heirlooms **'Early Golden Summer,'** **'Early Prolific Straightneck'** and **'Yellow Crookneck'** and compact **'Dixie'** and **'Sundance.'**

Winter squash recommendations include pumpkin varieties **'Jack O'Lantern,'** **'Kentucky Field'** and **'Sugar Pie.'** Try acorn types such as All American Selections winner **'Cream of the Crop,'** with white rind and golden flesh, or tasty green hybrid **'Table Ace.'**

Problems and Pests

Problems with mildew, cucumber beetles, stem borers, bacterial wilt and whiteflies can occur. Ants may snack on damaged plants and fruit, and mice will eat and burrow into squash for the seeds in fall.

Don't worry if some of your summer squash are too mature or your winter squash are not mature enough. Cured summer squash will keep for a several months. Use them in baked goods. Use harvested immature winter squash immediately and stuff, bake or barbecue.

Strawberries

Fragaria

Features: spreading perennial; soft, bright green leaves; white, sometimes pink flowers; bright red, edible fruit **Height:** 6–12" **Spread:** 12" or more

Many of these plants, with their pretty little white flowers, spread vigorously by runners. Long shoots spread out from the parent plant, and small baby plants grow at the tips. Buy just a few plants and you'll have plenty of fruit-producing plants by the end of summer. Depending on sun requirements and fruiting time, strawberries are considered either short-day or day-neutral. Short-day (June-bearing) types produce lots of fruit in one crop during spring. Day-neutral strawberries (ever-bearers) deliver spring through fall.

F. vesca

Starting

Use transplants and put them in the ground according to strawberry type and climate. Where winters are cool, plant short-day types in spring for next-year harvest; plant ever-bearing varieties in spring for summer and fall harvest. Where winters are warmer, plant short-day berries in fall for a spring crop; plant ever-bearers in spring and fall for three seasons of berries.

Growing

Strawberries grow well in **full sun** or **light shade**. The soil should be **fertile, neutral to alkaline, moist** and **well drained**. To avoid soil-borne diseases, do not plant them where tomatoes, egg-plant or peppers have grown in the past three years. Compost to enrich the soil.

You can avoid many problems by using drip irrigation. It keeps the shallow roots moist but not soggy. Drip irrigation also keeps the fruit dry so it is less likely to rot.

Harvesting

For the sweetest fruit, pick strawberries when their shoulders have turned from white to red. They will not continue to ripen once removed from the plant.

Tips

Strawberries make interesting, tasty and quick-growing groundcovers. They do well in containers, window boxes and hanging baskets.

Recommended

F. chiloensis (Chilean strawberry), *F. vesca* (wild strawberry, alpine strawberry) and *F. virginiana* (Virginia strawberry) have been crossed to form many hybrids. Similar in appearance, they generally form a low clump of three-part leaves and may or may not produce runners. Flowers in spring are followed by early to mid-summer fruit. Some plants produce a second crop in fall, and others produce fruit all summer. Fruit of wild or alpine strawberries is smaller than the fruit of the other two species.

Popular short-day strawberries include the large, flavorful **'Chandler'**; disease-resistant **'Guardian,'** particularly good in colder areas; dark red, long-fruiting **'Pajaro'**; and popular, disease-resistant, long-producing **'Sequoia.'** For ever-bearing types, check out the delicious, disease-resistant **'Albion'**; delicious, long-bearing **'Fern'**; popular, runner-producing **'Quinnalt'***;* and tasty, heavy-producing **'Seascape,'** which also resists diseases.

Problems and Pests

The fruit is susceptible to fungal diseases, so mulch to protect it. Some leaf spot, spider mite problems and wilt can occur. Snails, earwigs and sowbugs love strawberries.

Sunflowers & Sunchokes

Helianthus

Features: daisy-like, yellow, orange, red, brown, cream or bicolored flowers, typically with brown, purple or rusty red centers; edible seeds; edible tubers
Height: 6–15' **Spread:** 1–4'

The *Helianthus* family includes the familiar, cheerful, multi-seeded sunflower as well as the less well-known sunchoke. With its delicious, crunchy seeds, sunflower makes a wonderful companion for other seed-bearing plants such as amaranth and quinoa. A native species, sunchoke (Jerusalem artichoke) is grown like a potato for its edible tubers. It tastes like an artichoke or waterchestnut and is delicious cooked and mashed or sliced raw in salads. Jerusalem artichokes produce tall, yellow flowers.

Starting

Sunflowers and sunchokes can be sown directly into the garden in spring around the last frost date. Water well until the plants become established. Sunchokes are perennial and will grow back each year as long as you leave some of the tubers in place in fall.

Growing

Sunflowers and sunchokes grow best in **full sun**. The soil should be of **average fertility, humus rich, moist** and **well drained**, though plants adapt to a variety of conditions.

If you can't find sunchokes at the nursery, look in the grocery store. Plant 1.5" chunks with at least one eye. Plant sunchokes where you'll enjoy them for many years. They spread by underground runners and are potentially invasive.

Harvesting

Sunflower seeds are ready to harvest when the flower has withered and the seeds are plump. You may need to cover the flower heads with a paper bag or net to prevent birds from eating all the seeds before you get to them.

Sunchoke tubers are usually ready to harvest in fall. Store them in a cool, dry, well-ventilated area.

Tips

Sunflowers make a striking addition to the back of the border and along fences and walls. These tall plants may need staking in windy or exposed locations.

Sunchokes can be boiled, baked, fried, steamed, stewed or eaten raw. They cook more quickly than potatoes and become mushy if overcooked.

Recommended

H. annuum (sunflower) can develop a single stem or many branches. The large-flowered sunflowers usually develop a single stem. Many of the ornamental sunflowers offered in gardening catalogs have edible seeds. **'Russian Mammoth,'** a tall cultivar with large, yellow flowers, is one of the most popular for seed production.

H. annuum (photos this page)

H. tuberosus (sunchoke, Jerusalem artichoke) is a tall, bushy, tuberous perennial. It grows 6–10' tall and spreads 2–4'. Bright yellow flowers are produced in late summer and fall. Try **'Nakhodka'** or **'Waldspinel,'** which are both productive varieties.

Problems and Pests

Plants are generally problem-free, but keeping birds away from the seeds until they are ready to be picked can be troublesome.

Sunchokes store energy in the tubers as a carbohydrate called inulin. Because the energy is not readily absorbed by the body and does not affect blood sugar levels, these tubers are useful for diabetics and dieters.

If you don't mind sharing the seeds, sunflowers are a great way to invite birds into your garden. An added bonus: the birds will feast on garden pests while snacking on seeds.

Tarragon

Artemisia

Features: perennial with narrow, aromatic leaves; airy flowers **Height:** 18–36"
Spread: 12–18"

The distinctive licorice-like flavor of tarragon lends itself to a wide variety of meat and vegetable dishes and is the key flavoring in Bernaise sauce.

Starting

French tarragon, the tastiest tarragon, is started only from plants; you'll find them at nurseries, garden centers and specialty growers. Any seeds you locate are likely for the less-flavorful Russian tarragon.

Growing

Tarragon grows best in **full sun**. The soil should be **average to fertile, moist** and **well drained**. Tarragon spreads by creeping rhizomes. Divide the plant every few years to keep it vigorous and to encourage the best leaf flavor.

Harvesting

Pick leaves as needed or dry or freeze them for later use.

Tips

Though not very decorative, tarragon provides a strong accent. Try it in an herb garden or mixed border and let surrounding plants support its tall stems.

Recommended

A. dracunculus var. *sativa* is a bushy plant with tall stems and narrow leaves. Airy clusters of insignificant flowers are produced in late summer.

Problems and Pests

Tarragon rarely suffers from any problems.

Before purchasing a plant, chew a leaf to see if it has the distinctive French tarragon flavor. Russian tarragon (A. d. var. dracunculoides*) is more vigorous but has little of the desired flavor.*

Thyme
Thymus

Features: shrubby perennial with bushy habit; fragrant, decorative foliage; purple, pink or white, summer flowers **Height:** 8–16" **Spread:** 8–24"

A member of the mint family, this popular Mediterranean herb is used in soups, stews, casseroles and roasts. Place it where passersby can brush against it to release the pleasant fragrance.

When in bloom, thyme is a bee magnet. Pleasantly herbal thyme honey goes very well with biscuits.

Starting

Common thyme can be started indoors from seed four to six weeks before you plan to plant it outdoors. Purchase seedlings at nurseries and garden centers and from specialty growers.

Growing

Thyme does well in **full sun** or **partial shade** in warmer areas. The soil should be **neutral to alkaline** and of **poor to average fertility**. Good drainage is essential. Thyme tolerates drought once established.

Harvesting

Pick leaves as needed or dry for later use.

Tips

Thyme is useful for sunny, dry locations at the front of borders, between or beside paving stones, on rock walls and in containers. Once the plant has finished flowering, shear it back by about half to encourage new growth and to prevent it from becoming too woody.

Recommended

T. x *citriodorus* (lemon thyme) forms a mound of lemon-scented, dark green foliage. The summer flowers are pale pink. Cultivars with silver- or gold-margined leaves are available.

T. vulgaris (common thyme) forms a bushy mound of fragrant, dark green leaves. The summer flowers may be purple, pink or white. Cultivars with variegated leaves are available.

Problems and Pests

Thyme rarely suffers from any problems, but its roots can rot in poorly drained, wet soils.

Tomatoes

Lycopersicon

Features: annual vine; bushy upright or trailing habit; fragrant foliage; yellow flowers; red, pink, orange or yellow, edible fruit **Height:** 18"–5' **Spread:** 18–36"

Tomatoes…where to begin? There's a size and flavor for every garden, from tiny currant tomatoes to half-pound heirlooms. Once you taste a freshly grown tomato, store-bought never seems quite good enough.

Tomatoes grow well throughout California as long as the type matches the climate. They are heat lovers and thrive in sun. Where warmth and sun are less available, choose short-season tomatoes.

Starting

Tomatoes can be started indoors six to eight weeks before the last frost date. A large choice of seedlings is available from nurseries and garden centers.

Growing

Tomatoes grow best in **full sun**. The soil should be **average to fertile**, **humus rich**, **moist** and **well drained**. Keep tomatoes evenly moist to encourage good fruit production. Be careful not to overwater, as it dilutes the flavor. Avoid wetting the leaves to reduce the spread of disease. Except for the very small bush selections, tomatoes get tall and rangy. Use tomato cages or stakes to corral them.

Harvesting

Pick fruit when it is ripe. Tomatoes pull easily from the vine with a gentle twist when they are ready for picking.

Tips

Tomatoes have attractive little flower clusters and vibrantly colored fruit. Many of the selections grow well in containers and do well in patio gardens and hanging baskets.

Recommended

L. lycopersicum are bushy or vine-forming annuals with pungent, bristly leaves and stems. Determinate plants grow to a specific height and may not need staking. Indeterminate plants continue to grow all summer and into fall until killed by disease or frost; they require support. Clusters of yellow flowers are followed by fruit from mid-summer through to the first frost. Fruit ripens over a four to six week period to red, orange, pink, yellow or purplish black and comes in many shapes and sizes. Beefsteak tomatoes are the largest; currant are the smallest. Browse through seed catalogs to see the many offerings available. Try a few each year until you find your favorites.

When tomato plants were first introduced to Europe, they were grown for their ornamental value and not for their edible fruit. Tomatoes were once known as love apples because they were thought to have powers as an aphrodisiac.

When shopping, look for initials AVF-NTSt. They indicate disease resistance to the following: **A**lternaria Stem Canker, *Verticillium* wilt, *Fusarium* wilt, **N**ematodes, **T**obacco mosaic virus and **St**emphylium gray leaf spot.

The following varieties do well throughout California:

Cherry: **'Sungold,'** an early ripener with a heavy crop; **'Super Sweet 100 Hybrid VF,'** with reliable red fruit clusters; and **'Yellow Pear,'** with low-acid, mild, pear-shaped fruit.

Container: **'Better Bush Hybrid VFN,'** an early-ripening determinate type; the extremely compact **'Patio Hybrid VASt'**; All American Selections winner **'Small Fry VFNASt'**; and the very early-ripening **'Toy Boy VF.'**

Standard: the large, intermediate **'Champion Hybrid VFNT'** and abundant **'Early Pick Hybrid VF.'**

In northern and other areas with short or cool summers, try standard varieties **'Bingo VFT,'** a flavorful determinate;

heirloom semi-determinate **'Carmelo VFNT';** and early determinate **'Valerie VFN.'**

Problems and Pests

Problems with tobacco mosaic virus, aphids, fungal wilt, blossom end rot and nematodes can occur.

Tomatillos (Physalis ixocarpa) are related to tomatoes, and the plants have similar cultural requirements. The fruit is encased in a delicate papery husk. It is ready to pick when the husk is loose and the fruit has turned from green to gold or light brown. Tomatillos are the basis for many Spanish dishes and make a particularly great green salsa.

Turnips

Brassica

Features: biennial grown as an annual; clump of edible, blue-green foliage; plump, edible root **Height:** 10–18" **Spread:** 6–8"

Tender with a delicate flavor, these fast-growing Mediterranean natives should be eaten as soon as they mature for the best-tasting roots.

B. rapa

Starting

Where winters are cool, sow in early spring or summer. In warmer areas, plant in fall. Keep the seedbed moist until plants germinate. Several small, successive sowings will provide you with turnips for a longer time.

Growing

Turnips prefer **full sun**. The soil should be **fertile, acidic, moist** and **well drained**. If the soil is deficient in boron, the roots may develop discolored centers. Work agricultural boron into the soil if needed.

Harvesting

Harvest leaves a few at a time from each plant and steam or stir-fry them. Harvest roots in about 75 days, when they are plump and ready; they have the best flavor and texture when young. Turnips do not store well.

Tips

Add small groups to borders where the attractive clumps of foliage will provide a good background for flowering plants.

Recommended

B. rapa (turnip, summer turnip) is a biennial grown as an annual. It produces white or purple-shouldered, edible roots. The blue-green foliage is also edible. Try the popular **'Purple Top White Globe'** and unusual heirloom **'Rapa di Milano Colletto Viola.'**

Problems and Pests

Cabbage root maggots, cabbage white butterfly larvae, aphids, rust, fungal diseases, downy mildew, powdery mildew and clubroot are possible problems.

Turnips, originally grown as animal fodder, only became popular for dinner in the 1600s.

Watermelons

Citrullus

Features: annual vine; climbing or trailing habit; yellow flowers; decorative dark green striped, pale green skinned fruit **Height:** 12" **Spread:** 5–10'

Tasty and juicy, watermelon is the ultimate summer treat. These African natives love long, hot summers. Try a short-season early variety in cooler areas.

Starting

Watermelons require a long growing season and should be started indoors in individual peat pots four to six weeks before the last frost date. Started plants can also be purchased at garden centers and nurseries. Transplant into the garden after the last frost date once the soil has warmed up.

Growing

Watermelons grow best in **full sun**. The soil should be **fertile, humus rich, moist** and **well drained**. They like plenty of water during the growth and early fruiting stages. To intensify the flavor, use less water once the fruit is ripening. Give them room to spread.

Harvesting

A watermelon is generally ready to pick when the area where the fruit sits turns from white to yellow. Some people say ripe fruit produces a hollow "thunk" when tapped.

Tips

Small-fruited watermelons make attractive patio climbers, though they may need some support. These plants can be left to wind through ornamental beds and borders.

Recommended

C. lanatus takes 65 to 105 days to mature; the skin of the fruit may be a solid dark green or light green with dark green stripes; the flesh may be red, pink, orange or yellow. Popular early maturing cultivars include **'Golden Crown,' 'Sugar Baby,' 'Yellow Baby'** and **'Yellow Doll.'**

Problems and Pests

Problems with powdery mildew, *fusarium* wilt, cucumber beetles and sap beetles can occur. Watermelon fruit blotch is a serious problem that can affect this plant.

Watermelon is native to tropical parts of Africa, but it was introduced to Asia and has been grown there for centuries.

Glossary

Acid soil: soil with a pH lower than 7.0

Alkaline soil: soil with a pH higher than 7.0

Annual: a plant that germinates, flowers, sets seeds and dies in one growing season

Basal leaves: leaves that form from the crown, at the base of the plant

Blanching: to deprive a plant or part of a plant of light, resulting in a pale color and usually a milder flavor

Bolting: when a plant produces flowers and seeds prematurely, usually rendering the plant inedible

Bract: a special, modified leaf at the base of a flower or inflorescence; bracts may be small or large, green or colored

Cross-pollination: the pollination of one plant by a closely related one; undesirable if the resulting seeds or fruit lack the expected qualities; beneficial if an improved variety results

Crown: the part of the plant at or just below soil level where the shoots join the roots

Cultivar: a cultivated plant variety with one or more distinct differences from the species, e.g., in flower color or disease resistance

Damping off: fungal disease causing seedlings to rot at soil level

Deadhead: removing spent flowers to maintain a neat appearance and encourage a long blooming season

Diatomaceous earth: an abrasive dust made from the fossilized remains of diatoms, a species of algae; the scratches it makes on insect bodies causes internal fluids to leak out, and the insects die of dehydration

Direct sow: to sow seeds directly into the garden

Dormancy: a period of plant inactivity, usually during winter or unfavorable conditions

Double flower: a flower with an unusually large number of petals

Drought resistant: can withstand drought for a long time

Drought tolerant: can withstand drought conditions, but only for a limited time

Genus: a category of biological classification between the species and family levels; the first word in a scientific name indicates the genus

Half-hardy: a plant capable of surviving the climatic conditions of a given region if protected from heavy frost or cold

Harden off: to gradually acclimatize plants that have been growing in a protected environment to a harsher environment

Hardy: capable of surviving unfavorable conditions, such as cold weather or frost, without protection

Humus: decomposed or decomposing organic material in the soil

Hybrid: a plant resulting from natural or human-induced cross-breeding between varieties, species or genera

Inflorescence: an arrangement of flowers on a single stem

Invasive: able to spread aggressively and outcompete other plants

Loam: a loose soil composed of clay, sand and organic matter, often highly fertile

Microclimate: an area of beneficial or detrimental growing conditions within a larger area

Mulch: a material (e.g., shredded bark, pine cones, leaves, straw) used to surround a plant to protect it from weeds, cold or heat and to promote moisture retention

Neutral soil: soil with a pH of 7.0

Node: the area on a stem from which a leaf or new shoot grows

Perennial: a plant that takes three or more years to complete its life cycle

pH: a measure of acidity or alkalinity; soil pH influences availability of nutrients for plants

Plantlet: a young or small plant

Potager: an ornamental kitchen garden, often laid out symmetrically with raised beds or low, hedge-edged beds

Rhizome: a root-like, food-storing stem that grows horizontally at or just below soil level, from which new shoots may emerge

Rosette: a low, flat cluster of leaves arranged like the petals of a rose

Runner: a modified stem that grows on the soil surface; roots and new shoots are produced at nodes along its length

Seed head: dried, inedible fruit that contains seeds

Self-seeding: reproducing by means of seeds without human assistance, so that new plants constantly replace those that die

Single flower: a flower with a single ring of typically four or five petals

Spathe: a leaf-like bract that encloses a flower cluster or spike

Species: the fundamental unit of biological classification; the entity from which cultivars and varieties are derived

Standard: a tree or shrub pruned to form a rounded head of branches at the top of a clearly visible stem

Subspecies (subsp.): a naturally occurring, often regional, form of a species, isolated from other subspecies but still potentially interfertile with them

Taproot: a root system consisting of one long main root with smaller roots or root hairs branching from it

Tender: incapable of surviving the climatic conditions of a given region and requiring protection from frost or cold

Tuber: the thick section of a rhizome bearing nodes and buds

Understory plant: a plant that prefers to grow beneath the canopies of trees in a woodland setting

Variegation: foliage that has more than one color, often patched, striped or bearing leaf margins of a different color

Variety (var.): a naturally occurring variant of a species

Index of Plant Names

Boldface type refers to main entries.

About the Authors

Freelance writer and Master Gardener **Jennifer E. Beaver** discovered a passion for plants after witnessing their transformative power in neighborhoods. She helped found a group that successfully saves urban landscape trees, thereby reducing pollution and preserving property values. Captivated by the delights of container gardening, she is always on the prowl for new plant combinations to fill re-purposed containers.

Alison Beck has gardened since she was a child. She has a diploma in Horticulture and a degree in Creative Writing. Alison is the co-author of several best-selling gardening guides. Her books showcase her talent for practical advice and her passion for gardening.